Quick Steps to
Resolving Trauma

Also by Bill O'Hanlon

A NORTON PROFESSIONAL BOOK

Quick Steps to Resolving Trauma

Bill O'Hanlon

W. W. NORTON & COMPANY
New York • London

For information about permission to reproduce selections from
this book, write to Permissions, W. W. Norton & Company, Inc.,
500 Fifth Avenue, New York, NY 10110

For information about special discounts for bulk purchases, please contact
W. W. Norton Special Sales at specialsales@wwnorton.com or 800-233-4830

Manufacturing by RR Donnelley, Bloomsburg
Production manager: Leeann Graham
Digital Production: Joe Lops

Library of Congress Cataloging-in-Publication Data

O'Hanlon, William Hudson.
Quick steps to resolving trauma / Bill O'Hanlon. — 1st ed.
p. ; cm.
"Norton Professional Book."
Includes bibliographical references and index.
ISBN 978-0-393-70651-2 (pbk.)
1. Post-traumatic stress disorder—Treatment. I. Title.
[DNLM: 1. Stress Disorders, Post-Traumatic—therapy.
2. Psychotherapy, Brief—methods. WM 172]
RC552.P67O33 2011
616.85'21—dc22

                                        2010031965

ISBN: 978-0-393-70651-2 (pbk.)

W. W. Norton & Company, Inc.
500 Fifth Avenue, New York, N.Y. 10110
www.wwnorton.com

W. W. Norton & Company Ltd.
Castle House, 75/76 Wells Street, London W1T 3QT

1 2 3 4 5 6 7 8 9 0

To Helen
who knew the quick steps to my heart

Contents

Quick Steps to Resolving Trauma

Introduction:

Four New Approaches to Resolving
Trauma Briefly and Respectfully

Some years back, I was watching the television coverage of the third anniversary of the 9/11 attacks. The news channel CNN was interviewing some mental health expert about what the victims and those indirectly affected could expect to feel in the years to come, in reaction to that terrible day. He said, "These people will never get over this."

I had a very visceral reaction to this statement. First, I got angry. The "expert" was wrong. I knew it from my clinical experience as a psychotherapist who has worked with trauma for 30-plus years. And I was familiar with the professional literature on trauma that says he is wrong as well. People *do* get over trauma. People *can* get over trauma.

That moment of watching television led to the writing of this book. After I got angry, I became determined— determined to spread the idea that people could get over trauma, and that there are several new, innovative approaches to help them do precisely that.

I had been teaching seminars on the topic of trauma for several years at that point. While there are a lot of books and seminars available on the subject, none of them reflect or mention the ways that my clients and I have discovered that have worked for many of them. While nothing works for everyone, of course, because people are all unique individuals, and varied in their responses, I have found that a number of my clients have responded well to some or all of these methods, which will be discussed in more detail throughout the book.

> *Nothing is as dangerous as an idea when it is the only one you have.*
> —*Emile Chartier*

Most of the books on treating trauma are based on traditional, pathology-based views and methods. These approaches focus on the damage that was done to people and on navigating the long, difficult road to recovery that these "damaged" people face. Those traditional approaches often take years to work. They can be very hard on clients and patients as well as on therapists (there is a whole literature on "secondary and tertiary trauma" examining how therapists are traumatized by hearing about and working with severely traumatized people).

Interestingly enough, while I was preparing this book, I became immersed in the study of brain plasticity, inspired by psychiatrist Norman Doidge's amazing book, *The Brain That Changes Itself.* The view that I learned in undergraduate-level psychology courses at university turned out to be wrong in a significant way. It was thought in those days that after childhood, brains did not develop new brain cells or undergo any major new structural changes during the mature stages of life. However, research on brain plasticity carried out in recent years has shown that the brain continues to change and evolve throughout the life span. This is both good news and bad news in terms of trauma and its successful treatment. The good news is that successful trauma treatment is possible, because we know brains can change and adapt (within limits, of course), which should provide hope for therapists and clients alike as they work to adjust to life after trauma. By within limits, I mean that not everything in the brain can change in infinite ways. There are some structural limits as well as damage that cannot be repaired. But this brain plasticity can be a double-edged sword. I learned that whatever a person repeats creates neurological grooves in the brain—that is, the brain adapts to a continually repeated pattern, eventually accepting it as the norm. One of the implications of this finding is that focusing on the trauma over and over to treat it—which is the basis of almost all therapeutic approaches to treating trauma—may inadvertently be burning the trauma more deeply into the brain circuits.

I come out of a "resource" orientation to therapeutic change, strongly influenced by the work and attitudes of the late psychiatrist Milton H. Erickson. Erickson viewed people as resourceful, even admiring their symptoms as skills (albeit gone awry in their application), and drew upon their abilities for change more than trying to ferret out and correct their deficits and pathologies. So when I began to treat larger numbers of trauma clients in the 1980s, I learned traditional approaches to trauma treatment and didn't find them congruent with my view and approach. My clients and I developed the approaches you will read about in this book over time. Those clients taught me more than most of the training I had. Clinical results are a cruel and wonderful teacher. Either people feel better or they don't. Either their functioning improves or it doesn't. I recommend you take the same rigorous approach to the approaches offered in this book. Read about them, learn them, and try them out with a variety of clients. Use what works. Discard or modify what doesn't. Too much clinical work shows loyalty to theories and ideas over clients.

This book offers four alternate approaches to treating trauma. While not minimizing the damaging short- and long-term effects trauma can have, or denying the existence of posttraumatic problems in some cases, the book nevertheless offers a hopeful view that people can move on from trauma relatively quickly, when that trauma is approached in one of these four therapeutic ways. These approaches do not focus on the past, or on reliving trauma over and over again in order to resolve it. They offer some different ways to respectfully approach and resolve trauma rapidly.

The four approaches are:

1. Validate/value, and include all aspects of the person;
2. Connect the traumatized person to a future of possibilities;
3. Change the pattern of the posttraumatic problem;
4. Reconnect the person in places where he or she has been disconnected (whether from the self, others, the world, or meaning).

Let me be clear at the outset. *These are not the only ways to resolve trauma.* Other methods are available and work some of the time. The four methods presented here are merely the ones that my clients and I have found work best for us, but they are uncommon pathways to healing in therapy. This book exists because I could not find another one that discusses these methods, and I thought they were important enough to share with both therapists treating trauma, and patients suffering from trauma, in hopes that they would find these methods useful as well.

Myths and Misconceptions about Trauma and Treatment

Before we get into those four approaches in depth, there are some myths and misconceptions that many people, including

therapists, have about trauma and post-traumatic stress disorder
that I would like to address.

MYTH #1: ALL PEOPLE WHO SUFFER TRAUMA DEVELOP POST-TRAUMATIC STRESS DISORDER (PTSD)

We're not going to devote a lot of time or space to the
problem of the aftereffects of trauma here, since this is a book
on the successful treatment and resolution of the problem, but
let's get on the same page to start. The *Diagnostic and Statistical
Manual of Mental Disorders (DSM-IV)* (soon to be out in version
V) of the American Psychiatric Association provides a commonly
accepted description and set of criteria for what has come to
be called "posttraumatic stress disorder." Post-traumatic stress
disorder describes a set of symptoms that can follow exposure
to an extreme traumatic stressor involving direct personal
experience of an event that involves actual or threatened death
or serious injury, or other threat to one's physical integrity;
witnessing an event that involves death, injury, or a threat
to the physical integrity of another person; or learning about
unexpected or violent death, serious harm, or threat of death
or injury experienced by a family member or someone else to
whom one is close. The person's response to the event must
involve intense fear, helplessness, or horror (in children, the
response must involve disorganized or agitated behavior). The
typical symptoms include persistent reexperiencing of some
aspect of the traumatic event. People might avoid things that
remind them of, or are associated with, the trauma. They often
become hypervigilant (continuously scanning their environment
for potential threats) or hyperaroused (having an amplified, out
of the ordinary response) emotionally. They might also become
numbed in some key areas of their life, perhaps losing interest in
their careers, hobbies, or loved ones (or they may bounce back
and forth between extreme states of arousal and numbness). In
order to be clinically diagnosed with PTSD, they must exhibit

the symptoms for more than one month, and the symptoms must have a very significant impact, messing up their professional or home lives or relationships in a meaningful way.

The good news is that for years, PTSD wasn't recognized or acknowledged and now it generally is. The symptoms we  recognize today as PTSD have been present in veterans of war for a long time; in the aftermath of World War I, the condition was called "shell shock." It was initially seen (much like alcoholism) as a moral failing and weakness. However, as ex-soldiers of wars continued to suffer from these symptoms and appear traumatized, a more sympathetic view emerged. Eventually, parallels were drawn between the effects suffered by veterans and those observed in victims of rape, car accidents, child sexual abuse, and other major life traumas. From this, a picture of the typical aftereffects of unresolved trauma emerged.

However, as awareness of the newly recognized and named disorder spread, the general public and therapists began to get the impression that everyone who experienced severe trauma would necessarily develop PTSD. Research done in the past twenty years belies this common idea. Two studies that were done in the United States in the 1990s found that:

- 60.7% of men and 51.2% of women in the U.S. have experienced at least one traumatic event meeting DSM criteria;
- in Detroit, nearly 90% of residents have been exposed to traumatic events; but
- the general lifetime prevalence of PTSD is about 7.8% nationally and, for Detroit residents, is 9.2%. (Breslau, 1998; Kessler, Sonnega, Bromet, Hughes, & Nelson, 1995)

Another notable finding is that resilience seems to be learnable. Therapists who are treating war trauma have recently begun studying the most resilient soldiers to discover what strategies they use to cope, and then using that knowledge to help instill resilience in more vulnerable soldiers. Dr. Steven Southwick, himself a veteran of the Vietnam War, and deputy director of the Clinical Neurosciences Division of the National Center for PTSD, says this: "We do know there are factors that make some people resilient. There are genetic components to it, but there's a huge learning component. People can train themselves to be more resilient" ("Facing Combat Without Stress? Researchers Examine Most Resilient Soldiers," 2007).

MYTH #2: *PEOPLE WHO DEVELOP PTSD ONLY RESOLVE IT THROUGH THERAPY*

The clinical literature and the therapeutic community sometimes give the impression that, once a person develops PTSD, it will last forever unless it is treated with medication or therapy. Evidence shows, however, that PTSD often resolves without treatment—although treatment can help resolve it faster. This study found that people who developed PTSD showed a steep decline in symptoms over the first 12 months after it developed, followed by a gradual decline over 6 years. People who sought treatment experienced about half the duration of their PTSD symptoms than did non-treatment seekers (Kessler et al., 1995). So, there is a point to treatment, but we shouldn't give short shrift to people's natural healing abilities and resilience. People are often more resilient than we therapists give them credit for, perhaps because we so often hear about the most sordid aspects of life, and are so frequently exposed to the damage caused to our clients by trauma.

Bonanno, Rennicke, and Dekel (2005) found that expected rates of PTSD following the 9/11 attacks didn't materialize. Their conclusion: Resilience is "often the most commonly observed outcome" of exposure to potentially traumatizing events (p. 1). Others have found a similar surprisingly high level of resilience following trauma (Bonanno et al., 2002; Carver, 1998).

A recent study was the first to track large numbers of soldiers through the wars in Iraq and Afghanistan and provided an interesting glimpse into real-world data of rates of PTSD. Led by U.S. Navy researcher Tyler Smith and published in the *British Medical Journal*, the study monitored mental health and combat exposure in 50,000 U.S. soldiers from 2001 to 2006. The researchers took particular care to tie symptoms to types of combat exposure. Among some 12,000 troops who went to Iraq or Afghanistan, 4.3 percent developed diagnosis-level symptoms of PTSD. The rate ran to about 8 percent in those with combat exposure and 2 percent in those not exposed (Smith et al., 2008).

MYTH #3: *LONG-TERM, ABREACTIVE THERAPY THAT HELPS PEOPLE RELIVE AND ASSIMILATE THE TRAUMA IS THE MOST EFFECTIVE APPROACH*

As I mentioned above, this approach often takes years, and it is a hard row to hoe. Clients reexperience their traumas over and over again in an attempt to reconcile, reconnect, and move on. The first time was hard enough, but having to go through the trauma again, even with the support of a kind and skilled therapist, can be very challenging. Some people are unwilling to go through the process. Some deteriorate in their daily functioning during the course of treatment, often becoming more self-destructive (self-harming and suicidal). They might experience problems in their sex lives, or find themselves unable to trust friends or family members during treatment. All in all, though, if this were the only effective treatment, we would do our best to support people through the torturous process of remembering, reliving, and reexperiencing the emotions and sensations involved in the original incidents, knowing that in the end, the results would be worth it.

But I do hold that there are effective alternatives. That is the message and the point of this book. Research does not support the idea that one approach works for everyone. And it certainly doesn't support the idea that the abreactive, long-term approach to resolving trauma is especially effective in treating the aftereffects of trauma.

MYTH #4: *THERE ARE ONLY NEGATIVE EFFECTS FROM TRAUMA*

There is a whole literature on what has come to be called "posttraumatic growth," documenting the positive benefits that regularly follow trauma (Linley & Joseph, 2004). "In the developing literature on posttraumatic growth, we have found that reports of growth experiences in the aftermath of traumatic events far outnumber reports of psychiatric disorders." (Tedeschi & Calhoun, 2004, p. 1)

Tedeschi and Calhoun (1996, 2004) created the Posttraumatic Growth Inventory, an instrument for assessing positive outcomes reported by persons who have experienced traumatic events. This 21-item scale includes the factors New Possibilities, Relating to Others, Personal Strength, Spiritual Change, and Appreciation of Life. Using this instrument, they discovered that women tend to report more benefits than do men following trauma, and people who have experienced traumatic events that fit the *DSM-IV* criteria report more positive change than do persons who have not experienced extraordinary events. By this, I mean that they discovered that being exposed to very traumatic events made it more likely that people would report positive post-difficulty change. Those who had less extreme life disruptions usually weren't catalyzed into these major life shifts. "Reports of posttraumatic growth have been found in people who have experienced bereavement, rheumatoid arthritis, HIV infection, cancer, bone marrow transplantation, heart attacks, coping with the medical problems of children, transportation accidents, house fires, sexual assault and sexual abuse, combat, refugee experiences, and being taken hostage" (Tedeschi & Calhoun, 2004, p. 1) (If you are curious about this inventory, the American Psychological Association has it on their Web site: http://cust-cf.apa.org/ptgi/).

Sample statements from this inventory are below:

One is supposed to rate on a scale of 1–5 how much the trauma or crisis led to this:

I established a new path for my life.
I know better that I can handle difficulties.
I changed my priorities about what is important in life.
New opportunities are available which wouldn't have been otherwise.
I have more compassion for others.
I discovered that I'm stronger than I thought I was.
I have a greater sense of closeness with others.

This does not fit with the above-mentioned TV expert's statement of "They will never get over it." People do get over trauma, of course, but more than that, they sometimes thrive in the wake of trauma.

Of course, much of the time the aftermath of trauma is mixed, including both harmful and helpful elements. This book derives, in some ways, from an early trauma I experienced. I was molested when I was a boy, and the person who molested me used confusion to maneuver me into a position of vulnerability. Of course, this affected me in some negative ways and some of those negative effects still linger. But it made me wary of confusing situations and I developed an urgent interest in making things as clear as possible for myself and others through the ensuing years. That led to me becoming a workshop teacher and writer. People often remark on how clear my teaching is and my books are, and I believe this positive outcome can be directly traced back to the trauma I suffered.

I hope this book follows in that tradition and that you find it clear and accessible. And more than that, that the book makes a positive difference for you in your work, and in the lives of your clients or patients.

This book follows in the tradition of several of my previous books published by W. W. Norton & Company (*A Guide to Possibility Land, A Guide to Inclusive Therapy,* and *A Guide to Trance Land*), in that we have designed it to be consumed in bite-sized pieces, with whimsical graphical elements on the cover and throughout the book that make for a memorable  reading experience. It has been amusing for me to discover that people have been trying to make meaning from these graphics. They are generally random, so please don't spend your precious time and brainpower trying to figure them out. Just enjoy and learn.

Bill O'Hanlon
Santa Fe, New Mexico
March 2010

Inclusive Therapy: Reclaiming Devalued Experience

There is a perhaps apocryphal story in which a Scottish engineer, upon seeing his first steam engine, declared, "Well, it works in practice, but does it work in theory?" I'm pretty practical when it comes to clinical work and don't use much theory, but in the spirit of that story, I will offer a bit of theory in this chapter to orient us to trauma and treatment. Don't worry, it will be short and we will quickly move on to more practical matters.

There is a single overarching theory that organizes much trauma treatment, which has been called the *un-experienced experience* model of trauma. The idea is that, when people go through an extreme experience, they are so overwhelmed that they simply can't process it all. They separate from their feelings, their perceptions, their bodies, and their sensations. One writer on the subject puts it this way: "Simply, when something happens to us, we do not experience all of it at once. Experiencing is a process that takes place over time. It involves neurophysiological and somatic work on the part of the person to whom the experience happens" (Browne, 1990, p. 21).

The way to metabolize this un-experienced experience, in traditional psychotherapeutic approaches, is to have the person go back in time to the traumatic incident or incidents and relive them through remembering. With the support and guidance of the therapist, and in a safe environment, the person can connect with and more fully experience what was suppressed and put aside during the initial, overwhelming trauma. This is also called the *abreactive model*, in that people are encouraged to fully feel and often express the painful emotions involved in the original traumatic incident.

If you have ever used this approach with your clients, you will know that it usually takes some months, or even years, for the process to work. And during all that time, it is very difficult for the person reliving the trauma to revisit it so often—it was hard enough the first time; to go over it again and again is often tortuous. The therapist often finds the process a bit traumatizing to witness. The client or patient may deteriorate in their functioning in the midst of the process, sometimes becoming more self-destructive, self-harming, or suicidal. If sexual abuse was involved in the original experience, clients often find sex with their partners difficult, leaving their partners upset and sometimes unsupportive of the treatment.

Of course, if this were the only way to heal and move on from trauma, we would just have to do our best with these difficulties and carry on. Just as in addictions treatment, which for so many years relied on only one approach (the disease model and treatment based on 12-step groups), trauma treatment had one major approach. Not because it worked best, but because few alternatives were available. But, this book suggests that there are several alternatives to this traditional approach to processing the raw effects of the trauma.

The first method for doing this is a present- rather than past-oriented method I call Inclusive Therapy. Let me present a little theory and an analogy first to help you understand the Inclusive Therapy method.

> There seems to be some connection between the places we have disowned
> inside ourselves and the key to where we need to go. Life as usual has
> arranged a way in which we're not allowed to leave anything behind that is
> not somehow resolved.
>
> —David Whyte

1.0 The Phantom Limb: An Analogy for the Un-Experienced Experience Model

Sometimes, when people lose a limb, they still experience, sometimes in a painful or bothersome way, sensations in the missing limb.

In a similar way, aspects of the person who goes through trauma may be missing, cut off, from their conscious awareness, but still intrude upon the person at times. It's as if there is a longing for wholeness; those missing aspects want to connect to the whole person, but are not able to in the same way as before. If they can't find their way back in peacefully, they might crash into the traumatized person's life or experience in some disturbing form, such as flashbacks, self-mutilation, compulsive sexual acting out, or other things we in the psychotherapy world refer to as "symptoms." The cut off pieces might be sensations, perceptions, memories, feelings, or aspects of their "personality."

What follows is a visual representation of the process, with a little theory thrown in.

We all start life full of potential. Humans do most of their development after emerging from the womb. This

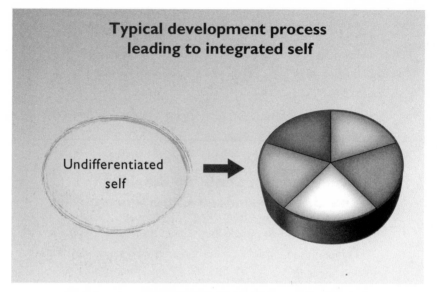

Figure 1.0.   Undifferentiated self to integrated self.

includes personality development. In our very early life, we don't distinguish ourselves very clearly from our environments and others. As time goes on, we start to coalesce into a coherent and relatively consistent "self" (Figure 1.0).

I call this the Integrated Self because the person experiences him- or herself as generally integrated and coherent, although they can still make inner distinctions. I am Bill, but I have different aspects of my experience and self. These are my emotions; these are my thoughts; this is my body. I am selfish as times, generous at others. But all these different things exist within the sense that I am Bill and these are aspects of Bill. I am Bill; I am separate from you and others; I am an individual. This Integrated Self is sometimes called the Identity Story, because it is largely constructed from gender training, attributions, cultural and family influences and narratives, and the things we tell ourselves and

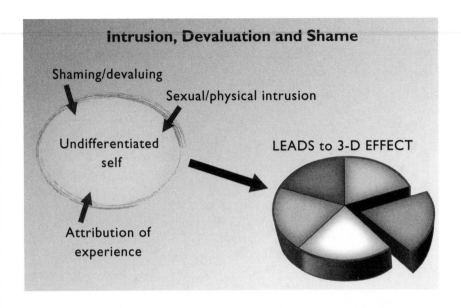

Figure 1.1.   Intrusion and trauma leading to 3-D effect.

believe about who we are. It's not "the whole truth and nothing
but the truth," but some selective aspects of the truth.

However, during this individuation and consolidation
process, some glitches occasionally occur. We get intruded
upon, both physically and psychically (Figure 1.1). Our
parents, and society, tell us what we "should" feel or what
we "really" think, even if it doesn't fit with our inner sense
of things, and we either get confused by this or take those
others' views or feelings on, reluctantly and uncomfortably.
We might also be physically abused or traumatized,
threatened, or hurt. We might be abused sexually, and
intruded upon in an unwanted and frightening or demeaning
way. We might experience the shock of the truly terrifying:

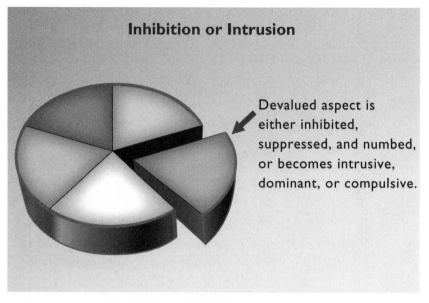

Figure 1.2.   Inhibition or intrusion.

the traumatic. These experiences can be overwhelming and leave us confused as to where we stop and others begin. These traumatizing others have intruded on our physical or psychic space.

In response, we sometimes "split off" aspects of ourselves or aspects of these troubling experiences (feelings, memories, sensations, and so on). This is akin to the phantom limb analogy used above. Some aspects of ourselves can go missing, or be excluded, in the aftermath of intrusive, shaming, traumatic experiences. These experiences can happen any time during life, but they seem to be the most disruptive to younger people who have not yet consolidated their sense of self. I call this splitting off process the 3-D process and will detail what I mean by 3-D shortly.

INHIBITION, INTRUSION OR BOTH

When some part of us goes missing, this manifests mainly in two ways: inhibition or intrusion (Figure 1.2). That phantom limb aspect of the self, that rejected and ignored part that hasn't been fully dealt with, is pushed aside, or our feelings about it are held back, or in some other way it is inhibited, thus limiting its full expression or presence in our lives. Some clients report that they can't recall much about their childhoods or about the specific traumatic incidents that have occurred in their lives. Some feel generally numb or hollow; they lose their meaning or connection to some specific aspect of their felt experience. Some sensations, such as sexual excitement, or a sense of taste, can become lessened. A key aspect of the person's personality might become diminished or less available to the person.

I once had a client who told me that her nickname growing up was "Sunshine." She was always seen to be happy. She was being physically abused within her family regularly, but showed no signs of that to anyone outside her family. Now, in her adult years, she found that she couldn't really experience anger fully when she was mad at someone or about something. If she tried to tell someone she was upset with them, she told them with a smile on her face and such a sweet voice that they didn't really understand how upset she was. Her phantom limb was anger. For whatever reason, she had disconnected from anger. She couldn't fully feel anger or express it effectively when needed.

Intrusion is the other common manifestation of the aftereffects of trauma. The split-off aspect of the person might become intrusive, showing up in unwanted, destructive, or unhelpful ways in the person's life. The person might act out sexually or might have intrusive,

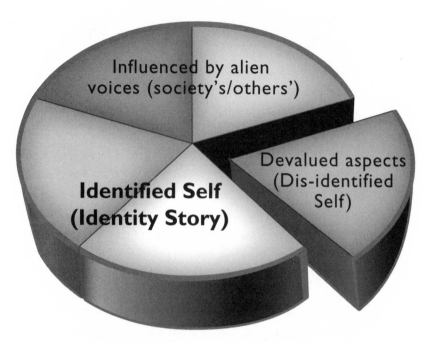

Figure 1.3.   Identified self and Dis-identified self.

unbidden flashbacks of some aspect of the trauma, such as smells or sounds experienced during the trauma. He or she might be reminded of the trauma by something in their present life, and suddenly feel as if he or she is back in the traumatic situation.

Of course, sometimes people will seesaw back and forth between inhibition and intrusion in the aftermath of trauma. My client Sunshine had several episodes in which she would explode in anger and begin to break things, frightening her children and herself. After such incidents, she would say things like, "I wasn't myself," and "I was beside myself"—and that is the typical experience of the phantom limb phenomenon. The person does not feel as if they are themselves when "taken over" by the missing aspect. They feel as if they have been intruded upon by something outside themselves—

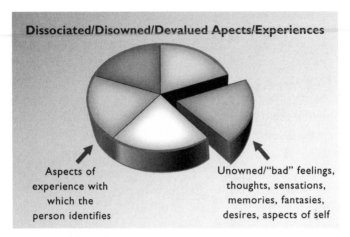

Figure 1.4.   The 3-D process.

something that they do not identify with, that is not part of their "identity story" (Figure 1.3). The missing aspect becomes an "it," not experienced or perceived as part of oneself. But it is part of oneself, just a dissociated, disconnected part that doesn't fit well into one's current conception of oneself. The aspect is seen as bad, evil, wrong, embarrassing, overwhelming, or frightening—in short, it is devalued.

This process of disconnecting could be called the "3-D" Process, where the three "D's" stand for Dissociated, Devalued, and Disowned (Figure 1.4). It's not a part of my experience (dissociated); it's not good or it's useless (devalued); and it's not me (disowned).

This is where the approaches put forth in this book deviate from the traditional treatment model. Instead of using a past-oriented, abreactive approach that involves reliving or reexperiencing the trauma, you will learn four alternate ways to bring the phantom limb back, or dissolve the posttraumatic problems. The first of these I call Inclusive Therapy. Using Inclusive Therapy to treat trauma aftereffects, we will be inviting the person to include, connect to, and gently begin to value and own the missing aspect of the self.

1.1 Three Levels of Inclusion

We use three levels of inclusion to make this invitation. These three levels are:

1. Permission
2. Inclusion of opposites
3. Exceptions

The following sections will detail each of these levels of inclusion.

1.2 Permission

The first level of inclusion involves giving the person permission to feel, experience, or be whatever it is that has been excluded and devalued or pushed away.

To do this, it is helpful to have a sense of what the "phantom limb" or the dis-identified aspect might be. For example, one of my traumatized clients was acting out sexually. She would feel numb when having sex with her fiancé, but found herself having sex with a relative stranger in an elevator and being quite sexually responsive during that encounter. I use the phrase "found herself" very intentionally, since she reported that she felt like she was acting on automatic pilot while the sex was beginning, and then she watched herself acting out the rest of this sexual encounter, and wondering why she was doing this. It was as if she were watching someone else have sex; she didn't feel like she was choosing or controlling her behavior.

For her, the phantom limb was "sexual arousal." As a young child, she had been abused by a cousin who had threatened her life while he was masturbating her to orgasm. This frightening and overwhelming experience was enough to lead her to disconnect from the powerful sexual sensations she was experiencing at the time of her abuse.

In this case, one could experiment with various permissions that might be helpful for this client.

We could try: *It's OK to be sexual.*

Or: *You can be connected and sexual.*

Now, neither of these may work. This method involves a process of experiment and response until we find something that begins to move the person. The individual may show relief; they may cry; their facial muscles may visibly relax; they may begin to talk about something they have never talked about or realized before. If the permission works, something shifts for the person experientially (and perhaps behaviorally).

There are two types of permission used in this level of inclusion: *Permission To* and *Permission Not To Have To*. A quick note here before we get into the details. These permissions are almost always about internal aspects of people (feelings, sensations, memories, thoughts, perceptions, or personality traits, for example). It can be dangerous, at times, to give permission for certain actions, such as anything that could be harmful to the person or to others. For example, we might give someone permission and validation for moments when they have suicidal thoughts or feelings, but not give them permission to actually harm themselves.

I'll illustrate:

Client: I get so discouraged, at times I think it would be better to just die.

Therapist: A lot of people think about dying to escape their pain. That option would make sense if there were no hope. And one of the reasons you came here was to find that hope.

One would not say:

Therapist: If you can't find hope, then you can take that option.

And one would not say:

Therapist: It's OK to kill yourself, but let's see if we can find a way to avoid that.

The first permission is targeted at the inner aspects of the person's experience, not their behavior.

THE LANGUAGE OF PERMISSION

The usual words and phrases we use in this method are listed below.

For the *Permission To* side of things:

You can
It's OK
You're OK if you
It's common
A lot of people feel/experience
You could

For the *Permission Not To Have To* side of things:

> You don't have to
> It's OK not to
> You're OK if you don't
> You might not

Again, to illustrate:

Therapist: You don't have to remember anything that you
    don't want to or need to remember.
Therapist: It's OK to feel numb.

So, let's examine this process of using permission in the treatment of trauma. These examples are taken out of context to illustrate the particular methods discussed in the section. Obviously, in treatment, things won't be broken up so much and many of these methods will be used in conjunction with one another.

By using permission, the therapist is trying to gently invite the missing elements that have been devalued and extruded to be allowed and included in the person's experience and sense of self.

Client: I have been drinking a lot to make myself
    oblivious so I won't feel the pain.
Therapist: It's OK to want to get away from
    the pain. Most of us would want to get away
    from or avoid pain. Is drinking working for
    you?
Client: Well, it does help me escape the pain for a while, but
    of course the drinking brings on other problems, so no, not
    really.

Therapist: So, the impulse to diminish or get away from the pain is a healthy one, but the way you have been going about it isn't working so well. I guess that is part of our task in therapy, then. To find other ways to decrease that pain so you don't feel so tempted to deal with it in destructive or unhelpful ways.

Client: I am up for that.

.   .   .   .

Client: I just dissociate whenever I feel frightened.

Therapist: It's OK to dissociate. That's one way to handle fear. There are other ways, now that you are away from the old environment where that was the only way you could find to deal with being overwhelmed. You can dissociate and you don't have to.

Client: It just happens. I don't seem to have much control over it.

Therapist: Sure. It's been happening automatically much of the time. I'm just saying I think there are some ways to diminish or stop dissociating when it's not serving you well. And that it is perfectly understandable, given what you've been through, that you would dissociate.

.   .   .   .

Client: I read this book that said the only way to heal from abuse was to remember everything and feel it all. That terrifies me. Frankly, I would rather die than do that. It was hard enough the first time. I don't want to go through it all again.

Therapist: Remembering it all and feeling it is one way to resolve things. And there may be other possibilities. You don't necessarily have to remember and feel it all to heal.

And I certainly understand not wanting to go through it all again. It sounds as if it was horrendous.

. . . .

Client: I hate to be so frightened and sad all the time. I wish I were like Mr. Spock; all rational and not so emotional.

Therapist: It's OK to be frightened. It's fine to be sad, even if you don't want to be. And you don't have to be frightened or sad all the time.

1.3 Inclusion of Opposite Possibilities

This is where things become a bit more complicated (and very interesting, too!). This level of inclusion gives people permission to feel two seemingly opposite feelings at the same time—or to be two seemingly opposite things at the same time.

In the wake of trauma, people often have contradictory feelings about or senses of themselves. They feel confident *and* weak. They feel present *and* stuck in the past. They often flip between these two feelings or states of mind.

With this method, we are inviting them to simultaneously experience these two contradictions, so that there is no switching or conflict between them. It's as if two aspects or feelings within the person are trying to get through a doorway that is too small to contain them both and they get stuck. This method creates a double door that allows both aspects to be expressed at the same moment, thereby (theoretically) dissolving the conflict.

The use of inclusion of opposites is especially helpful when people are conflicted, caught in dueling injunctions ("I have to

____ but I can't or shouldn't _____"), or are ambivalent. The
therapist is trying to gently make room for both sides of the
conflict or ambivalence and again, include them in the person's
experience.

Client: I am stuck.
Therapist: You can be stuck and move on at the same time.

. . . .

Client: My wife tells me I should just get over it. I tell her I
will never get over it and she gets really mad at me. At the
same time, I find myself having fewer nightmares and I am
getting less depressed.
Therapist: You'll never get over it and you are moving on.
Client: Yes, that's it. You never get over something like this
but you can move on and get better. Can I write that
down and tell it to my wife the next time we have this
argument? She needs to understand that when you go
through something like this, you never get over it. But
maybe it would help her calm down and have some hope
if she knew I was also moving on, even though I'll never
get over it.

. . . .

Client: I hate my father. And at the same time, he's my father. I
feel guilty and I guess in a way, I still love him even after all
that's happened.
Therapist: It's complex. You love him, you hate him, you
feel guilty. Is it okay to just let all that be and not have
to have it make any sense? Just to make room for all the
contradictions?
Client: I guess so. It's weird. But I could just hang out with the
mixture and see how things go.

> *Do I contradict myself? Very well, then I contradict myself; (I am large—I contain multitudes.)*
>
> —*Walt Whitman*

1.4.1 Oxymoron

An oxymoron is a phrase or figure of speech made up of two seemingly opposing or normally opposite words. The word "oxymoron" derives from the Greek roots *oxy-* which means sharp, and *-moron*, which means dull. The phrase "awfully nice" and the term "jumbo shrimp" are oxymorons. If you think about them, you'll notice they are rather strange; they contain words that contradict each other. Oxymorons can be used in this method of inclusion to express two opposite feelings or aspects of a person in one stroke. They can also be useful as inclusive phrases to validate, give permission for, or express two contradictory aspects or feelings clients may be experiencing.

Therapist: You can have an unconcerned vigilance that can keep you safer without draining your energy.

. . . .

Client: I feel like I'm broken.
Therapist: From what I've learned about you, you have kind of a broken integrity or as Leonard Cohen put it, "There's a crack in everything; that's how the light gets in."
Client: That's great. I do feel like somehow this brokenness has opened up something for me. Maybe I'm telling the truth about myself and my life for the first time in years.

. . . .

Therapist: So you do everything for everybody in an attempt
to get them to love you. Then they just take you for
granted. That's terribly accommodating of you.

Client: Yes, that's a good way to put it. Terribly accommodating.
It's great for them but terrible for me. Maybe I'll start to be
terribly unaccommodating for a change.

1.4.2 Apposition of Opposites

Another way to include opposites is to use a method called
"apposition of opposites." This is similar to the concept of
the oxymoron, but the words are used in the same sentence,
or near one another, rather than combined into the same
phrase.

Therapist: You can remember to forget those things that are
important to forget and remember to remember those
things that are important to remember.

Client: I think I need to stop holding on to all those
resentments. Maybe I can forget those things and finally let
them go.

. . . .

Therapist: You can feel bad about feeling good and good about
feeling bad. You could also feel bad about feeling bad and
good about feeling good.

Client: I so tired of feeling bad. I want to feel good.

He who confronts the paradoxical exposes himself to reality.

—Friedrich Dürrenmatt

1.4.3 Tag Questions and Comments

When I was studying with Milton Erickson, he once said to me, "If you can't say the 'no,' then the patient will say it." So, he used a method called tag questions in which he would include the "no" with the "yes." The method involves adding a negative phrase onto a more positive statement or question. Or, alternately, adding a more positive ending to a negative statement or question. He would say things like: "You really want to change this, do you not?" Or "You can't get over this easily, can you?" In this method, you are including the "no" without making it very explicit. You are saying "yes" and "no" at the same time.

Here are more examples that might occur in a therapeutic setting.

Therapist: You really want to remember what happened, do you not?

Client: My life is shattered.
Therapist: And all the king's horses and all the king's men, and no amount of therapy could put you all back together is how it seems, no?
Client: No, I guess in some ways I am getting better. It just seems like I have gone through so many terrible things, sometimes I get discouraged and think I'm screwed up for life. But I still have the sense that I can get better. That's why I'm here.

1.5 Exceptions

This is the third and final level of inclusion. In this method, we recognize and include the possibility that things are not always as we or our clients say they are or think they are. We recognize that life and people are more complex than they often initially appear.

Let me give you and example of this, which occurred spontaneously during a session with a client of mine who had been sexually abused during childhood. When she began therapy, she thought she was a terrible, unacceptable person and considered herself somehow to blame for the fact that she had been sexually abused. During the course of treatment, she came to see that the abuse was not her fault.

But in one session, in a whisper, she told me that she had something to say that she had never told anyone and about which she was very ashamed, but that she needed to tell it to me. Three times during her adolescence, she had deliberately sought out one of her abusers to have sexual contact with him.

My initial response to this was that she was blaming herself again. I offered some comfort and reassurance: She had been sexualized when young; she was dissociated and operating on automatic pilot; and so on. But she was having none of it. "Don't do that therapist thing, Bill. Excusing everything. Psychologizing everything. These were things I chose to do and I am ashamed of what I did. I want to take responsibility for them. If I was not responsible for choices I made, then none of my abusers were responsible for what they did either and that's not right. I feel very ashamed telling you this stuff, but I need to tell someone."

So, the message was: She was not responsible for her encounters with her abusers—except when she was. This is the essence of this level of inclusion.

Here are some other ways to conceptualize exceptions:

This is the way it is except when it is not this way.

I do brief therapy except when I do longer-term therapy.

I orient to solutions except when I don't.

The only way to heal from trauma is to relive the experience. Or not.

This level of inclusion helps recognize the complexity of situations and human beings.

Here are some examples of clinical dialogue exemplifying this approach.

Client: I always screw things up.

Therapist: Except when you don't.

Client: (Laughing) Well, yeah, there was that painting I sold last week for thousands of dollars. I guess that wasn't a screwup.

. . . .

Client: Every time I have a flashback, I cut myself to get away from the pain.

Therapist: Is there or was there ever a time you had flashbacks and didn't cut yourself?

Client: I never cut myself at work. And I have flashbacks there at times.

Therapist: What is different about work? How do you keep yourself from cutting yourself there?

Client: Well, everyone there sees me as strong and competent. I'm the one who has always got it together. I'm the calm in the eye of the storm. I like to be seen like that and wouldn't want to blow my image.

Therapist: OK, that is why you don't cut yourself when you have a flashback at work, but I am also interested in *how* you don't cut yourself. What do you do to manage the impulse or feeling or flashback?

Client: I get busy doing something productive that I can feel good about.

Therapist: Could you try something similar when you're at home? If a flashback comes, you get absorbed in some productive project as a way to break the association between flashbacks and cutting?

I don't have time to have time for everything. I don't have seasons enough to have a season for every purpose. Ecclesiastes was wrong about that. I need to love and to hate at the same moment, to laugh and cry with the same eyes, with the same hands to cast away stones and to gather them, to make love in war and war in love. And to hate and forgive and remember and forget, to set in order and confuse, to eat and to digest what history takes years and years to do.

—Yehuda Amichai

We have now reviewed the first of four methods this book offers to rapidly resolve traumatic aftereffects. This one, called Inclusive Therapy, involves gently giving permission and including, thus inviting the person to include the aspects of themselves and their experience that have been un-experienced or un-metabolized. In the next chapter, we will take up the second method: inviting the person to the future as a way of pulling them out of the past.

Future Pull: Did You Know that the Future Can Cause the Present?

Most trauma treatment orients people to the past, helping them go back to reclaim their missing experiences and resolve trauma by reliving it. But in this second method for resolving trauma, presented in this chapter, we will do the exact opposite. We are going to invite people into the future to help them move on from trauma.

Let's listen to Howard Lutnick, CEO of the financial services firm Cantor Fitzgerald, who lost his brother, his best friend, and 658 employees in the 9/11 attacks. He was not at the World Trade Center that morning because he was taking his child to his first day of school. Five years after experiencing the trauma of that day and all that loss, he said, "We always thought we'd fall apart at some point. I'd tell people it was like surfing in front of a very large wave and as long as I kept going forward as fast as I possibly could, the wave would never get me. But if I ever stopped, and took a moment to look back . . . Whoosh, the wave would crash over me, and I'd get crushed. But if I kept moving forward, the wave would get smaller and smaller, and that's what happened" (Barbash, 2006).

Now, you might think Lutnick is in denial, and that he *should* go back and face the tragedy head on, but this strategy is working for him—and it works for many of my clients, too. They prefer to orient to a future with possibilities and in which they have moved beyond the trauma, rather than going back to the past to relive or confront it.

I learned this approach from Milton Erickson. Sometimes, in therapy, things would not be going well with a particular patient. Erickson would put the patient into trance and suggest to them that time was changing. It was now one year since their last psychotherapy appointment. They were back for a follow-up visit to discuss all the positive developments that had occurred in their lives since therapy had ended. He would then ask them what he had done during therapy that they had found particularly helpful. After they told him about what therapy interventions had helped them, he would suggest they develop amnesia for all that they had told him. He would bring them out of trance and proceed to implement the interventions they had told him were so effective. It would usually work.

The point is that Erickson held the view that people had a blueprint for positive futures and change within them, and it was his task to evoke those blueprints and help the patient put them into practice.

Because so much trauma treatment is focused on returning to the past rather than going toward the future, we might inadvertently be imposing our biases and theories on our clients. They might be more adept at moving toward preferred futures, rather than revisiting painful pasts. The method detailed in this chapter provides several future-oriented interventions that can be used as invitations. If the client responds positively to these invitations, it might be an indication that this is their best pathway to change and resolution.

2.1 The Victor Frankl Strategy

I sometimes call this future-pull approach the Victor Frankl Strategy, because of an anecdote I heard about Frankl, the late Viennese psychiatrist, that illustrated this future method.

Frankl, imprisoned in several concentration camps during World War II by the Nazis, kept his mind and hope alive by rehearsing talks he would give after he was released from imprisonment. He had discovered a new idea: that purpose and meaning were central to mental health.

One freezing-cold winter day, while being forced to march outside the concentration camp, Frankl developed a coughing fit and found he could not continue walking to the work detail. He fell to the ground. A guard, frustrated by Frankl delaying the group's progress, began to beat him. Weakened by both the beating and the illness that had led to the coughing fit, Frankl collapsed onto all fours in the snow, certain he could not get up and move another step. The guard then threatened to kill Frankl right then and there if he did not get up and walk. Without his conscious intention, Frankl found that he was no longer in the field on all fours, but was transported in his mind to the future. He vividly imagined himself giving a lecture in post-war Vienna on "The Psychology of Death Camps and the Psychology of Meaning." He became so involved in this imaginary lecture that he no longer felt his current pain and debilitation. During this imagined speech,

he spoke about a harrowing moment during his time in the
concentration camps when he was threatened with death and
felt as if he did not have the strength to get up and save his
life. Then, wondrously, he found the strength, stood up, and
began walking. As he was imagining telling this to his audience,
his body arose in the field where he was on all fours outside
the concentration camp. He began to walk. He imagined this
talk all the way to the work detail and all the way back to the
concentration camp, finally ending the imaginary talk to an
imagined standing ovation.

I want to highlight what Frankl did and why I call this the
Victor Frankl Strategy. When he was traumatized, instead of
staying frozen in the traumatic experience, Frankl oriented to
a future without the trauma. A future in which he was in
a better, safer place. A preferred future. Then he used
that compelling and preferred future to pull himself out
of the difficult present. This last part is important, so
let me emphasize it. If Frankl had "escaped" to a better
future, it would have been merely a pleasant fantasy to
ease his pain while he died at the hands of a Nazi guard.
But Frankl's future influenced his present. You might say
that his imagined future caused his present.

Most of the time in therapy (and in most Western conceptions
of time and causality), we have the idea that the past
causes the present. I suggest that the future (or at least our
imagined future) can exert a great deal of influence on the
present.

What follows are some methods, less dramatic than Frankl's,
that can be used with people to invite them into orienting to
the future in order to resolve trauma.

2.2 Future-Pull Methods

What follows are some clinical methods of helping people connect to a hopeful and better future. You may not use all of these methods (or indeed, any of them; that is why I have provided four methods on the book, to give you flexibility based on a particular person's responses and preferences). Or you could use a combination of one or two. Please be guided by what works to get a good response. If there is no response, or a negative one, move on to some other approach.

2.2.1 Problems into Preferences

I sometimes call this method "Carl Rogers with a Twist," since it involves empathically reflecting back what your client is telling you, but introducing a future orientation in your reflection.

"With a twist" means that here we will not just be purely reflecting and summarizing what the client communicated, but adding a little bit of a twist (or a "spin," to use the current political phrase). In addition to reflecting respectfully the person's expressed or unexpressed feelings or experience, we are leading them a bit when we use this method. The leading is in the direction of connecting with a positive future.

2.2.1.a Rephrase From What is Unwanted to What is Desired

In this aspect of the method, restate and reflect what the person just told you that may be past-oriented or discouraging into what you imagine or sense they are longing for or might want, instead of what they are suffering from or complaining or discouraged about.

> **Client**: I've been dealing with this for years and I'm still stuck.
> **Therapist**: So you'd really like to get a sense that something we do will move you on.

> **Client**: I can't stop cutting myself. These flashbacks are really getting to me.
> **Therapist**: You'd like to find a better way to handle these flashbacks or have less of them.

2.2.1.b   Redirect From the Past to the Future

When people arrive in therapy, especially people who are troubled by or stuck in the past, they often speak about what they don't want in the past. This method subtly re-orients them by reflecting (again, with a twist), by rephrasing from the past and what they don't want to the future and what they do or would want. We are helping them move from complaints to longings; from problems to solutions; from pain to hope. But it is all done so subtly that most clients don't even consciously recognize the shift.

> **Client**: I feel like my whole life has been about my trauma.
> **Therapist**: You'd like to move toward a life that isn't determined or dominated by your past.

> **Client**: I've never been able to trust anyone.
> **Therapist**: You'd like to be able to trust someday.

2.2.1.c   Mention the Presence of Something Rather than the Absence of Something

This part of the Problems Into Preferences method involves mentioning something that person might like in their life rather than just getting rid of the unwanted experiences. If you find it too awkward to do this, you can mention the absence of the problem, so don't worry too much about it. But it is always nice to imagine something one wants in the future rather than just getting away from something painful.

Client: I rub my skin raw with an eraser every night. I rub swear words into my skin. Then I have to wear long sleeves, even on hot days. People think I'm weird.

Therapist: You'd like to treat your body with more care and feel less like a weirdo.

2.2.1.d   Suggest Small Increments Rather than Big Leaps

Sometimes people in therapy become discouraged because they haven't made big changes. Or, they don't believe they can change at all. This part of the method sets the expectations lower and orients to smaller positive changes that might seem more achievable.

Client: I can barely get out of bed. It takes me hours every morning.

Therapist: You'd like to get out of bed a bit quicker and find some more energy to get going at least some of the time.

Client: I just want to leave all this shit behind.

Therapist: You want to feel you have moved on from as much of the past as you can as fast as you can.

> *You have to go fetch the future. It's not coming towards you, it's running away.*
> —*Zulu proverb*

2.2.2 Expectancy Talk

This method involves creating an expectation of positive developments in the future by implying them through language. The therapist uses phrases and questions that create a sense of inevitability about positive or improved futures.

The therapist uses phrases and questions that contain words and phrases like:

How quickly?
Yet
So far
After
Before
When
Will

Of course, be careful what you presume. If you ask, "How quickly do you think you'll have your next relapse?" you are presupposing a negative, rather than a positive, better future.

Therapist: How quickly do you think this depression could lift, realistically?

Client: I don't know. I suppose if we found something that helped, it could lift pretty quickly, maybe in days or a week.

Therapist: And when you start to feel better and less depressed, who do you think the first person, other than you, will be to notice that change?

Client: The people at work. I would be more vocal in meetings and I would get to work on time.

Therapist: OK, so after you are out of this depression, people at work would notice. Who else?

Client: My brother. He is very sensitive and notices any little change in my mood.

Therapist: And what kinds of things would your brother notice when you are feeling better?

Client: My voice first, I think. He can tell over the phone when something isn't right or when I am in a particularly good mood.

Therapist: Okay, who would notice next?

. . . .

Therapist: So you haven't found a way to stop cutting yourself yet?

. . . .

Therapist: So far, nothing has diminished the flashbacks.

. . . .

Therapist: So, when the dissociation eases, you'll feel more connected to people and the world?

Client: Yes, I would be more myself around them. You know, funny and irreverent.

Therapist: And how have you been with others when you are more disconnected?

Client: Well, mostly I stay alone. But when I am with other people and feeling dissociated, I am just more quiet and in my head.

Therapist: So you will be more talkative when things are better?
Client: Yeah.

2.2.3 Investigating Preferred Futures

If you don't help clients challenge their default futures, that is, the ones that would come about if nothing changed, they are likely to end up with those futures in which their troubles continue. In this section, we are helping people discover and connect to futures in which the troubles that brought them to treatment are resolved and they are living lives they would prefer.

2.2.3.1 Working Backwards from the Future Without the Problem

This method involves exploring with the client what life might be like in the future, without the problem present any longer. In contrast to most trauma treatment, I often start an assessment with questions about what life will be like without the posttraumatic problems, when therapy is successfully completed.

I ask questions such as: When we are done with therapy and things are better, what will be happening in your life? What could you do, think, or focus on during the next while that would help you move a little bit in that direction, or would at least be compatible with it?

Another way to explore this problem-free or problem-resolved future is to ask what various parts of the client's life might look like without the problem. I ask variations on these questions:

- If your problem disappeared, what would be different?
- In your relationships?
- In your daily life?

- In your thinking or focus of attention?
- In your actions?
- In any other areas?
- Is there any part of that you could start to implement in the near future?

Therapist: When the nightmares and flashbacks stop, how will that shift your daily life?

Client: I would have more energy because I would be sleeping better at night. I would also have more time to exercise and be with my kids.

Therapist: Let's see if we can help bring some of that future into the present by finding any part of that you could start to do, even a little bit, in the next week or two. Could you commit to exercising at least 15 minutes every day? Or to spending at least five special minutes with each of your kids? Or both?

Client: I could spend some times with the kids. I think that might help them and me.

The future enters into us, in order to transform itself into us, long before it happens.

—*Rainer Maria Rilke*

Another method for starting from the place without the problem in the future is the Miracle Question, created by Steve de Shazer, the founder of solution-focused therapy. Here is the structure for asking the Miracle Question:

- Say: "Imagine that as you sleep tonight, a miracle occurs and the problem or concern that brought you to therapy is resolved." Make certain that the client is experientially involved in the scenario. When I first tried this method, it fell flat. Later, when I watched Insoo Kim Berg using it, a light bulb went off for me. She spent a lot of time helping the person get into the imagined scene, asking them to tell her where they would be sleeping that night, then asking them to imagine they went to sleep and a miracle happened. She kept checking in with the person to make sure they were following, not just intellectually, but experientially. After seeing that, the method worked much better for me.
- Ask: "When you first open your eyes, what is the first thing you notice that lets you know that this miracle has occurred?"
- Ask: "How would other people know the miracle had occurred? What would they notice that is different about you or what you are doing?" Again, don't move on until you are sure they are really engaged experientially.
- Keep tracking the changes through the day, the week, the month, and so on.

Here's a sample dialogue using the Miracle Question.

Therapist: I am going to ask you what you may think is a strange question. Imagine you go to sleep tonight and your posttraumatic problems are resolved by a miracle while you sleep. Just gone.

When you wake up tomorrow, what would be the first thing you would notice that told you that the miracle had occurred, since you were asleep and wouldn't be aware of it until you woke up?

Client: I wouldn't have this heavy feeling in my heart.

Therapist: OK, no heavy feeling. What feeling would be there instead?

Client: Maybe happiness or peace.

Therapist: Happiness or peace. OK. And what will you do
    differently when you have happiness or peace in your heart?

Client: Probably go spend time with my son, just playing with
    him and watching him or reading to him.

Therapist: And how would you son know that
    things are different and better with you?

Client: Well, he would probably notice that I
    am smiling more. And I would use a softer
    voice with him.

Therapist: And how do you think you using a
    softer voice and smiling more would affect him?

Client: He would probably be happier and less fussy.

Therapist: And if he were happier and less fussy?

Client: I would probably give him more attention.

Therapist: And how would that affect your day?

Client: I would be more relaxed and feel closer to my son.
    Maybe I could try deliberately speaking more softly. That
    might work.

Therapist: It's worth a try.

And so on. The therapist can keep exploring and following this
thread as the day unfolds. Just by eliciting this description, often
it becomes more present for the person. Or, as in this case,
they get inspired to bring some of this imagined future into
the present or near future. Sometimes they arrive at the next
therapy session reporting that they did many of the things they
described after the miracle occurred in this imagined scenario.

2.2.4 A Letter from the Future

Another potentially useful method is to encourage your client
to write a letter to him- or herself from his or her future self.
Obviously you are suggesting that they write a letter from a future
in which things are better and their major issues are resolved.

Here are the guidelines for composing such a letter:

- Have the person write a letter from their future self to their current self from a place where they are happier and have resolved the issues that are concerning them now.
- Have the future self describe where they are, what they are doing, what they have gone through to get there, and so on.
- Have the future self write about the crucial things they realized or did to get there, or write about some crucial turning points that led to this future.
- Have the future self give the present self some sage and compassionate advice from the future.

Therapist: I'd like you to try something I think might be helpful. Write a letter to your present self from a future self that got through all the things that have been troubling you and brought you to therapy. It could be from six months, or one year, five years, or even ten years in the future, whatever time you feel is right. In this letter, what would your future self say about where you are and how you got there? What were the major turning points that helped you resolve the issues and move on? What kinds of things are you doing in that future? And, if your future self could give you some comfort or wisdom from that future or some good advice, what would they say? Spend some time writing and revising this letter and bring it in to our next session, if you would.

Here is one such letter:

Dear Maggie,
*   I am writing to you from your future. You see, I am you. Your future self.*
*   Don't worry. You will make it through this troubling time. Have faith. Don't*
give up on yourself or life.

Things got better soon after you received this letter. You began to accept yourself as imperfect but not a bad person. You stopped drinking finally, not just cut back, because you finally realized that drinking never leads to anything good in your life. That helped a lot of things. You began to care for your physical health, getting back into aerobics and spin classes. You cleared out all that mental and physical gunk from your system. You began eating a healthier diet.

You also cleared out all of Bob's stuff, donating it or throwing it away. You burned the most hurtful items. That felt sad but good.

You ended therapy on a good note, feeling healthy and hopeful for the future. This future was worth living for. You have love and good friends.

Trust yourself. Keep the faith. You go girl.

A hopeful future can be a powerful antidote to a painful past. As Abraham Lincoln said: "The best thing about the future is that it comes only one day at a time."

A Real-World Example of Future Pull

Here's a practical example of the application of this future orientation. A psychiatrist in England named Elspeth McAdam was asked to see a 14-year-old girl who had been abused when she was younger and was now angry and refusing to go to school. The girl had a shaved head covered with tattoos, and looked as if she hadn't showered for some time. She seemed very angry about being sent to another in a series of shrinks, all of whom had failed to get her back in school. But Dr. McAdam just said, "You've talked to everyone about your past. I'd like to hear about your dreams for the future." The girl's whole face lit up when she said her dream was to be a princess.

"What kind of a princess would you be?" asked Dr. McAdam. "A people's princess," replied the girl, "who would be kind and generous and a beautiful ambassador." When they explored this idea a bit more, it turned out that the princess was a social worker who helped others.

"OK," said Dr. McAdam, "it is now 10 years later and you are a social worker. What university did you go to?" The girl mentioned one in the north of England.

"And what did you study?"

"Oh, I don't know, psychology and sociology and things like that."

"And since you went to university, that must mean you graduated from secondary school. You'd been out of school for two or three years. How did you get back in school?"

"I had this psychiatrist who helped me."

"How did she help you?"

"She made a phone call to the school and we met with the headmistress and I got back in."

"Who spoke when the call was made? You or the psychiatrist?"

"The psychiatrist."

They continued talking about what that meeting was like for some time and then moved on to other topics. After another month of meeting together, the girl said one day, "I think it's about time we went to the school, don't you? Will you make that call?" Dr. McAdam made the call and when they met with the headmistress, the girl was very appropriate and convincing. She was taken back into the school and eventually graduated.

It was ten years later that the girl became a social worker.

2.3 Something Waits for You After This: On Being a Suicide Counselor in a Death Camp

Victor Frankl, whom I mentioned earlier, was the suicide counselor in one of the death camps in which he was imprisoned during World War II. Jews who had heard rumors about the death camps and didn't believe them would often be so devastated when they arrived at one of them and saw the grim reality, or when they saw one of their family members shot in front of them while they were helpless to do anything, that they would indicate to one of their fellow prisoners that they intended to kill themselves. There was a relatively effective way to do so. It was called "going for the fence." The prisoner would run toward the electrified fence surrounding the camp. Either the guards would shoot him or the electricity would kill him.

Frankl was asked on occasion to speak to such a person and try to talk him out of it. He reported that his most effective method was to tell the person some variation on the message: *Don't do this. Something waits for you after this.*

But when Frankl was liberated from the camps, he discovered that his mother, his wife, and his father had all perished in the camps. He made his way back to his house, only to discover that it had been taken over by others who refused to move out.

He had no job, little food, and no money. He thought to himself bitterly: *All those people I told that something awaited them after this. Nothing was waiting for me.*

 But actually, within a year or so, Frankl became the head of a medical clinic in Vienna, found a place to live, and met his future wife. Something had awaited him after all.

A hopeful future can be a powerful antidote to a painful past.

In the Shape of a Bottle: Changing Patterns that Were Shaped by the Trauma

3.1 Introduction to Changing Posttraumatic Patterns

One of the notable characteristics of posttraumatic problems is the repetition of experience and behavior. People seem stuck in some sort of groove, with portions of their upsetting experience repeating endlessly, seemingly beyond their control. It is like a train that just keeps going around and around on a circular track. One way out of this repetitive loop is to pull the lever that sends the train on down the line by changing the repeating pattern.

Behavior, feelings, thoughts, actions, perceptions, memories, and neurological patterns can persist in the wake of trauma. They keep repeating long after the precipitating event has occurred. In this chapter, we will examine some methods for helping people change posttraumatic patterns.

3.2 Pattern Intervention: Patterns vs. Set Realities

In order to understand and accept that the interventions in this chapter (and in the whole book, I suppose) can work, you need to accept that things that appear to be set realities are in fact merely established patterns that repeat, and thus appear to have more solidity than they actually possess.

Consider this analogy. Cancer seems to be
a "thing." It is something that people "have"
or "get." But cancer researchers trying to
help people with that diagnosis think about
it differently. They break the thing called
"cancer" into process components and
try to intervene in any part of the process to resolve, treat, or
prevent the problem. Some of them target the genetic pathways
that give rise to or influence the development of cancer. They
try to change the expression of genes or do gene therapy. Other
researchers target the growth of blood vessels that cancer cells
need to grow so rapidly. Shutting off the growth of new blood
vessels for a time can inhibit or slow cancer growth. Still other
researchers conduct research that seeks to prove that cancer can
be prevented through nutritional interventions or exercise.

I think of traumatic problems in a similar way. Posttraumatic
stress is not a set thing, but a process with various repetitive
elements, any of which could be changed to prevent, shift, or
resolve trauma.

In this chapter we will try to find patterns related to the post-
trauma problem that we can change, and to discover whether
that helps diminish the posttraumatic suffering and increases
positive posttraumatic functioning.

3.3 The Doing of Traumatic Patterns

We will especially focus on shifting those thought patterns or
processes that are under the influence of the person suffering
from post-trauma problems, and the therapist. I sometimes
think of this as the "doing" of posttraumatic stress. I don't mean
this in a blaming way, but as a way of describing which parts of
the problem we can "get to."

3.3.1   Get People to Teach You How You Could Reproduce the Problem if You Tried to Create It

In this method, we are asking people to describe their problems in terms of things they could do (or we could do) to create the problem if we deliberately tried to make it happen. This accomplishes a couple things: it gives us a handle for changing the pattern of the problem, and it helps people start to think of their post-traumatic problems as changeable. Often people feel as if these problems just come over them or happen. Using this method, they can begin to imagine they have some influence on the occurrence of the problem.

Therapist: If I were going to cut myself, as you said you have, how would I go about it?

Client: Well, first you would get real depressed; then you would start thinking of all the terrible mistakes you have made. Then you would feel as if you deserved to be punished. Then you would get out an eraser and start rubbing it on your skin to make a mark. When the mark was dark enough and rubbed into your skin enough to see, you would get a pin and start scratching over the marks until you started to bleed. Then you would feel numb and hopeless.

.   .   .   .

Therapist: Teach me your method for getting depressed.
Client: I don't get what you mean. It just comes over me.
Therapist: Well, I know the feeling of depression just happens, but if you could teach me the things that you have control over and that make it more likely that you would get depressed, what kinds of things are those?

Client: I don't do anything? Are you saying I like to be depressed?

Therapist: No, not at all. It's just that you have told me the medications you are taking only do so much. And I am searching for something that you have some influence over that might help, even a little.

When I was in college, I got very depressed. I was not eating well at the time. I was pretty isolated, spending hours alone. And I spent a lot of time brooding about the past and comparing myself to other people–I always seemed to lose the comparison.

That's the kind of stuff I mean. Looking back, I think I could have made a little more effort to connect with other people–calling my family, making dates to meet with friends, that kind of thing. I could have experimented with drinking less cola–I tended to get revved up and then crash after about 8 cokes each day and then I would be up half the night with the caffeine in my system.

Anything like that you could think of that is under your influence and might make a difference in your depression levels?

Client: Yeah. Yeah. I am pretty isolated too. Maybe I could make a point of calling my best friend at least once a week. That might help.

3.3.2 Get Details of the Thoughts, Feelings, Sensations, Fantasies, Actions, Interactions, and Contexts When the Problem Typically Happens

Here we are trying to find details of the inner and outer patterns surrounding or involved in the post-traumatic problems. This again can give us a handle on where to intervene in the pattern.

Therapist: Tell me what kinds of thoughts go through your mind just before you have a flashback.

Client: First I just get scared and overwhelmed. Then
   I think about my abuse. Pictures just flash into my mind.
   Then I feel disgusted with myself. And then I start
   cutting.

. . . .

Therapist: What do you notice in your experience as you are
   getting anxious?
Client: Like someone is punching me in the stomach. I can't
   catch my breath. And my stomach hurts.

3.3.3 Get the Client to Imagine What Bodily Processes Are in Play When They Have Their Problems

This is another method of finding aspects of the posttraumatic problem pattern that might be available for pattern
intervention.

Therapist: If you had control of all the body's physiological
   functions, how would you create this problem?
Client: If I were going to do a good anxiety attack, I would
   increase the body's heart rate and increase sweating in the
   hands.
Therapist: And if you were to decrease the
   heart rate and the sweating, what would
   you do?
Client: I guess I could take a cool shower.
Therapist: This may seem a little crazy, but could
   you try that the next time you are getting anxious?
   What we are trying to do is to change the patterns of
   anxiety.
Client: Wow, I never thought of that. It might work. I would
   love to have something other than medications, which don't
   always help if the anxiety is high enough.

Client: I have this feeling of stabbing pain in my back. It feels
   like the knife that he was pressing into me during the
   attack. I know it's not real, but it feels real.

Therapist: Okay, let's see if we can get a handle on this and
   maybe shift it in some way. Sometimes if you experience
   some other sensation on that same pathway that gives
   you the stabbing pain, it can interfere with the stabbing
   feeling. Could you think of anything that could use the
   same back sensation area and give a different message to
   your brain?

Client: I have this back massaging chair that might work. You
   sit in it and little bumps move around and "massage" your
   back.

Therapist: Okay, it might not work, but it might. Give it a try
   and let me know.

3.3.4 Ask the Client How They Would Make the Problem Worse or Better, If They Could

This gives a message that the problem could be, at least in part,
under the person's influence, and also gives a possible place for
pattern intervention.

Therapist: If I were going to learn how to make the insomnia
   even worse than it is, what would I have to do if I were
   you?

Therapist: Is there anything you have done that seems to help
   you go to sleep and stay asleep?

3.4 Neurology: The Fast Track Out of Trauma

I had been a therapist working with trauma for many years when some radical new approaches to resolving trauma appeared on the scene: Eye Movement Desensitization and Reprocessing (EMDR) and Thought Field Therapy (TFT). These controversial approaches (the American Psychological Association would not endorse continuing education for TFT and related approaches at the time of this writing, and some prominent therapists have attacked EMDR) have claimed rapid and positive results working with even long-standing and previously treatment-resistant trauma. Since their introduction, several other similar approaches have been put forth. Let me give you an overview of these approaches, and then offer my explanation for why they work when they do.

3.5.1 The Eyes Have It: EMDR

The most well-known of these relatively new approaches is EMDR, or Eye Movement Desensitization and Reprocessing. This approach was first "discovered" by its founder, psychologist Francine Shapiro, while she was walking in the woods near her Northern California home. She happened to think of some trauma from her earlier life and was momentarily overwhelmed by the flood of emotions that accompanied the memory. Then something strange occurred. Dr. Shapiro's eyes began to move rapidly back and forth (so-called saccadic eye movements, which occur during the REM, or rapid eye movement stage of sleep) and as they did, she noticed she became less and less upset. Soon, she found she could think about this previously upsetting memory with almost no emotion. She thought the change must be related to those eye movements, so she deliberately thought about another upsetting memory and tried the eye movements. Again, they worked.

Soon she was trying this with her patients. She found that people could rarely do the eye movements on their own, so she began to guide the movements with her fingers. Gradually she worked out a procedure that seemed to work with most of her trauma and phobia patients.

She connected with the local veterans' hospital and began to set up preliminary experiments to research the efficacy of this procedure more scientifically, a process that is still going on in many settings, yielding mixed results so far, but showing some promise and evidence for effectiveness.

However, the enthusiastic acceptance from therapists and counselors didn't wait for the research. Thousands of them have taken one- or two-weekend-long courses (Level I and Level II) offered by the organization Francine Shapiro set up to provide her officially sanctioned trainings, emoria.org. Many have reported amazing, seemingly miraculous clinical results. I won't take a stand one way or the other on what the science will say ultimately; we'll have to wait and see. But I include it here because I think it points to something broader than EMDR in the successful treatment of trauma.

The procedure is relatively straightforward, although the reader is reminded that it should be done in the context of a good assessment and a strong working alliance with the client, and never beyond the scope of one's competence (for example, one wouldn't, even after taking the official EMDR trainings, work with complex dissociative disorders without having more training specifically in treating dissociative disorders).

A short summary of the main aspects of the EMDR process is given below (again, if the reader is interested, it is important to get some training and supervision before using this procedure, and to inform clients of the experimental and unproven status of the method). This is the way I learned it and the "protocol," EMDR's official version of the treatment process, has probably changed since then and will change in the future. Practitioners who specialize in EMDR and true believers will insist that the latest version is the "right" one, but there is little scientific proof for these claims. Francine Shapiro helped many people long before the current version was in place, after all, and before there were any Level I and Level II trainings available.

1. Identify a traumatic memory from the past or a current feeling, image, sensation, or symptom that is posttraumatic as a target for the intervention.
2. Have the client briefly focus on the target feeling, image, sensation, or memory.
3. Get a baseline rating from the client on 3 scales, going from 0 to 10 (10 being the most intense):
   a. How upsetting is the image, memory, sensation, or feeling on that scale?
   b. How intrusive or vivid is the image, memory, sensation, or feeling on that scale?
   c. Identify some negative or unhelpful self-talk, belief, or idea the client has or had about the traumatic incident at the time or now. Have the client rate on that scale how much they believe the idea or self-talk right now. (Use a 1 to 7 scale here.) (If possible, have them identify an alternate belief that would be more helpful or self-affirming. You may have to help them

articulate or formulate this alternate belief before or
during the procedure.)

4. Do the desensitization procedure by moving your finger
rapidly back and forth in front of the person's eyes about
21 times (experiment to find their optimum number).

Find a comfortable distance from their eyes about level
with their gaze. Alternate procedures include tapping in
a rapid alternation on the person's knees, clicking your
fingers rapidly in one ear and then the other, or different
hand movements (in a diagonal, in a figure eight, etc.). The
main factor for effectiveness seems to be rapid bilateral
stimulation in one of the sensory modes (sight, touch, or
hearing) while focusing on the trauma or some anxiety or
posttraumatic symptom. You may talk and encourage the
person to keep moving through the experience, and you
may also help them consider that new, more helpful belief.
They may speak and describe what is happening or they
may remain silent during the procedure.

5. Stop and tell them to clear their minds of the image or
feeling. Between procedures you can stop and check the
current rating scales on the three measures taken during
the baseline reading. Ask them if they have anything else
to report. Discuss, make adjustments, and reassure them
as needed.

6. If they are agreeable to continuing, continue the
procedure until they have a significant drop in the rating
toward the lower numbers on the scales. Check with
them between each series of 21 movements.

7. As the numbers on the three scales drop, have the client
rate how much they now believe the more helpful self-
talk or belief on a scale of 1 to 7. That number should
begin to go up toward 7 as you continue the procedure.
You can gently suggest they consider the new belief or
give them affirming messages while you are doing the

procedure to help them integrate it when they are in the change state induced by the procedure.

Sources of controversy surrounding EMDR are:

1. Is the treatment effective?
2. Are the results due to the placebo effect or hypnosis? If it is effective, are the eye movements or bilateral stimulation active ingredients of the effectiveness of the treatment, or is something else responsible for the results?
3. Shapiro's organization keeps a tight rein on who receives the training (only licensed mental health practitioners) and tries to limit the dissemination of the material (ostensibly for quality control concerns, but some people feel the emphasis is more on the control part of that equation). They claim that it is unethical for people to use the procedure without specifically attending one of their trainings.
4. If it is unethical to treat people without having attended one of their trainings, who did originator Francine Shapiro practice on before there were such trainings? Was she being unethical in her previous use of the method?
5. Neurolinguistic programming (NLP) practitioners claim that Shapiro derived the method from NLP and had training in their procedures, which include eye movement changes as part of their repertoire of treatments. She has reportedly said that NLP had no influence on her "discovery."
6. If this method has a neurological effect, as has been claimed, why is a therapy license required to attend the official trainings? Shouldn't its use be limited to neurologists and neuro-psychologists?

As I said, the scientific jury is still out on EMDR (and even more so on the methods I will discuss in the rest of this section, which have even less research evidence for their effectiveness), but those of us who work with people who are suffering want the latest and most effective methods, and so the therapeutic community generally is not waiting for science. If EMDR and the other methods I discuss can help even one of our clients, we want to use it sooner rather than later.

You can find more information, including a summary of much of the research on EMDR, on the EMDR Web site (www.emdr.com). You can also write to the EMDR Institute at P.O. Box 51010, Pacific Grove, CA 93950–6010, call them at (831) 372–3900, fax them at (831) 647–9881, or e-mail them at inst@emdr.com.

3.5.2 Tapping Into Resources: Energy Therapies (TFT, EFT and Others)

Next up is Thought Field Therapy (TFT), and the subsequent therapies following in its footsteps, the best-known of which is EFT (Have you noticed that all of these procedures are known by initials? That seems to be a requirement, at least as far as marketing goes, to have one's procedure become well known. Don't worry, I'll explain all the initials as we go).

TFT was created (or "discovered") by Roger Callahan, a California psychologist. As I understand it, he had learned some alternative medicine methods, including applied kinesiology (or "muscle testing") and acupressure. He began to investigate whether these would help in his therapy work. He specialized in working with phobias, using mostly behavioral and hypnotic methods. He found out about one set of acupuncture points that, when stimulated, were said to reduce anxiety and fear and tried them out on one of his most phobic clients.

After attending some training in this acupuncture-based method, he returned to his practice and his most challenging phobic patient, Mary. Mary had a fear of water. She had rated standing on a diving board above the swimming pool outside Dr. Callahan's home office as a "10" on a scale of fearful things, 10 being the highest level of anxiety.

During the course of a year-long treatment, they had been able to slightly reduce Mary's fear levels, but she still couldn't go near any standing body of water without severe anxiety and panic.

Dr. Callahan explained to her that he had learned a new treatment method and she agreed to try it out. He asked her to think of standing on the diving board above his pool and then tap some points right under her eyes as she felt the anxiety start to rise. She started tapping and then exclaimed, "I can't feel the anxiety any more!" Dr. Callahan said, "Okay, take a minute and re-focus until you can get the anxiety back and we'll start again."

"No, Dr. Callahan, you don't understand. It's gone. The fear is gone!" With that, she ran out of his office door. He followed, perplexed at first, but then alarmed as he saw her run to the diving board and begin to bounce happily on the end of it, right above the water.

"Mary," he called, now becoming a little anxious himself, "be careful. You know you can't swim."

"I know that, Dr. Callahan. It's just such a wonderful feeling, being free from that sick feeling in my stomach."

The procedure worked so rapidly, he was astonished. After working with the woman for over a year with only minimal results from his usual methods, he was able to help her resolve her phobia in a few minutes in one session with the acupuncture methods.

Callahan asserts that, in emotional as well as physical illness, energy along the body's energy meridians (those channels of energy that Chinese Medicine believes course through the body, bringing life and vitality to the body and the spirit) gets blocked (this is held to be true in traditional Chinese medicine as well). Focusing on the trauma or emotional upset brings the "thought field" to the foreground, where it available for treatment by stimulating the relevant points on the body.

He went on to develop the procedure further, discovering other points on the body that could be tapped or rubbed to help both reverse resistance and rapidly resolve traumas, phobias, and even depression and addiction. He claims an 80 to 95 percent success rate, depending on the level of training achieved and tools used by the therapist. Callahan also claims that most people can be successfully treated in only one session. These claims have led him and some of his followers to run afoul of professional therapy organizations, most notably the American Psychological Association, which has recently balked at approving CEU (continuing education unit) credits for any workshop that teaches the procedure.

Nevertheless, clinicians by the thousands have been trained in the so-called energy therapy methods, of which Callahan Techniques, as he calls his version these days, is one. Since

Callahan charges quite a bit for his training and is sometimes viewed as a bit difficult, others have developed their own variations of his method and have called them by different names, often charging less for training.

Here I will describe one, called Emotional Freedom Technique (EFT—see, I told you I'd explain the initials), created by Gary Craig. The nice part about this procedure is that it is both a self-help treatment (meaning you and your clients can use it on your own) and that Craig has generously offered both a free manual you can download from his Web site (http://www.emofree.com), as well as a free video (well, you do have to pay shipping costs) showing you the procedure. So, I am inclined to steer you toward him, if you are intrigued by this procedure.

Here, in a nutshell, is the procedure of EFT:

1. Find a trauma, fear, or other problem to focus on. The focus can either be a memory or a current symptom (flashback, craving for addictive substance or activity, anxiety, and so on).
2. Have the person rate how upset they are on a scale of 1 to 10 when focusing on it.

3. Do muscle testing to find out whether the person is resistant. You can bypass this if you pre-treat for resistance by a specific tapping, rubbing, or breathing method before you do the main procedure. (This is too complicated to explain here—go get the manual if you want to learn more). But this step is crucial. If the person is resistant (in energy therapy jargon, "reversed"), the process will not work.
4. Apply the main treatment by having the person tap various acupuncture points.

5. Have them tap another point on the back of their hand (the "gamut" point) while opening and closing their eyes, rolling their eyes in circles, counting and humming out loud (again, see the manual or go to a training to learn the details).
6. Have the person re-tap the original acupuncture points.
7. Check the number on the 1 to 10 scale. It should now be at or near 1. If it isn't, repeat the treatment or re-treat the resistance.

You can find the free manual, get a low-cost video, and more on Craig's Web site: http://www.emofree.com.

Again, why should this relatively brief and simple method work? And what does it have in common with EMDR and other similar methods?

Read on. I'll detail a few more methods and then the pattern they share will be illuminated. And it will teach us something fundamental about trauma treatment.

Sources of controversy surrounding this technique are:

1. Is the treatment effective?
2. Callahan and some who use his treatment claim a high success rate without having the hard research evidence to back up such claims. One psychologist has been reprimanded and punished by his state licensing board for making these kinds of claims.
3. There are many brands of this approach, some of them are quite complex, and they make competing claims for their effectiveness as compared to other Callahan-derived methods (they go by names like Getting Thru Therapy [GTT], Be Set Free Fast [BSFF], Emotional Diagnostic and Treatment Methods [EDxTM], and

Whole-Life Healing [WLH]. More initials, eh?). How are clinicians supposed to know which training to take or which method to use?

4. Chinese medicine practitioners, acupuncturists, and chiropractors, rather than therapists, seem to have the appropriate background and training to use and refine these treatments since they are based on alternative health methods and Chinese medicine. Is this method beyond the scope of therapists' and counselors' training and expertise?

3.5.3 Hold It Right There: TAT

Tapas Fleming is a California-based (why do so many of these new treatments originate in California, I wonder?) doctor of Oriental medicine (O.M.D.) who developed a procedure that, instead of using eye movements or tapping, involves merely holding some acupuncture points on the face, and holding the flat of one's hand on the back of the head as a treatment for trauma (she also uses it as a treatment for allergies). It is called Tapas Acupressure Technique, after her name, or TAT. The idea behind TAT is similar to that of TFT and EFT: opening up blocked energy as a way to rapidly resolve trauma.

The steps involved are:

1. Select a target memory or symptom.
2. Get a rating (on a scale of 1 to 10) on the severity of the problem.
3. Hold points on the face and hold the back of the head for a minute or so.
4. Watch for change or distress.
5. Get new ratings on the scale.
6. Repeat as necessary (especially with new positive cognition and focusing on where things related to the trauma or problem have been held or experienced in the body).

7. Drink lots of water after the treatment to help the
   system clear.

You can find out more details about conducting this process
from Fleming's Web site: http://www.tat-intl.com.

3.5.4 **3-D Glasses: SCtD**

Finally, the last method is one called Shifting Consciousness
through Dimensions, or SCtD. It was created by a man named
Lee Cartwright, in Santa Fe, New Mexico (finally we made it out
of California!).

Cartwright noticed that each of the procedures detailed
above focused on only one aspect of how people experience
the world. As a trained body worker, he had observed that
people function on three planes or dimensions in the physical
world: right and left (as in EMDR); up and down (as in TFT
and EFT); and back and front (as in TAT). He decided to
use all three and found he could often help people who
didn't respond to a particular approach by switching to
another dimension. He found he could often get hints about
which dimension to use by observing the person's gestures,
language, or movements while they were speaking about the
problem. For example, someone might only use their
left hand, moving it up and down, while describing the
problem. This might suggest that getting the person to
move in the right-left dimension and stimulating the
back and front dimensions could be a good starting
place. Or if the person said something like, "The
memory is right in my face and I'd like to put this all
behind me," activating the back dimension would be
warranted. Cartwright's method might explain why each
of the other approaches seems to work sometimes, but not

always. Because people may be "stuck" post-traumatically in one particular dimension of experience (right-left; up-down; back-front), some interventions would work for that person and others wouldn't. He has tried to increase the success of these interventions by both being more precise and more comprehensive: More precise in assessing which dimension might be involved in the problem, and more comprehensive in including all the dimensions.

Here is a brief description of the SCtD method. As with the other methods, summarizing it in such a short space does it a disservice and, if the reader is interested, he or she should contact Cartwright to receive training or buy some of his training manuals. He can be reached via e-mail at LeeCartwright@yahoo.com.

1. Select the target memory or symptom.
2. Assess the client by watching movements as the person speaks about the target,
3. Stimulate different dimensions (right/left; up/down; front/back) by touch, tapping, movement, or awareness shifts (that is, have the person focus on the target while shifting his or her attention to the back and front of the body, or right and left, or up and down).
4. Reassess and/or shift focus or dimensions.

In addition to alerting you to some new trauma treatment developments, I devoted so much space to them because I think their commonalities point to something profound about treating trauma effectively. What do all these procedures have in common and why do they work? My explanation has little to do with "energy," meridians, right and left brain integration, and the other explanations that the practitioners and originators of these approaches offer.

Instead, very simply, I think these interventions change the neurological pattern of the trauma. Performing these tappings, eye movements, skin stimulations, sounds, etc. changes the neurological patterns and grooves the trauma keeps settling into. They can work so rapidly because trauma seems to reside not only in behavior, thoughts, feelings and memories, but also in neurology (of course, behavior, thoughts, feelings, and memories have their neurological correlates as well).

Since our neurology processes things so quickly (probably due to a need to assess and process things quickly to help us survive), changing neurological patterns can work very quickly.

3.6 Perceptual Methods for Rapidly and Painlessly Resolving Trauma

It seems to me that the next most rapidly effective methods for resolving trauma are the perceptual methods.

I had a colleague who would regularly have clients who were experiencing flashbacks begin to systematically substitute different sensory elements within the intrusive memories. For example, he would have the person imagine that everyone in the flashback scene had just inhaled helium and talked in high-pitched Mickey Mouse voices. Or, he would instruct them to put a blue-colored overlay on the whole scene. Or, the person would make the scene into something that appeared as though one were looking at it through the wrong end of a telescope— very far away, and very small. He found these "perceptual" pattern interventions effective in reducing the occurrence of the flashbacks and their emotional valence.

There are two oft-used perceptual intervention strategies in NLP (neuro-linguistic programming) that have been found useful in treating persistent traumatic symptoms. I will describe them here.

Visual-Kinesthetic Dissociation with Visual Sub-modality Changes as Trauma Resolution Method

1. Identify a representative traumatic memory from the past as a target for the intervention.
2. Have the person visualize themselves in black and white on a screen as they are sitting in a movie theater. [The first level of dissociation]
3. Then have the person imagine floating out of their body and watching themselves sitting in the movie theater watching the screen. [The second level of dissociation]
4. Then have the person watch themselves watching a movie of the representative traumatic experience, ensuring that they go all the way to the end of the incident (that is, to a time when they were no longer frightened or upset after the incident).
5. Then have the person run the movie backwards, very rapidly, in color and step into the image before it runs. Note: Make sure they hit an end point for the backwards movie or they could just loop through it again and again. Have them run it several times, watching to see their physical response, which will probably be quite noticeable the first few times and then diminish rapidly.
6. Then check the results of the procedure by having the person focus on the incident or asking them to imagine something that would re-evoke the traumatic response and both notice and ask them how they felt during this revisiting. If they still have the traumatic response, repeat the procedure and try altering some of the visual submodalities you didn't have them change before (perspective, depth, etc.).

The Swish Technique

1. Identify a representative traumatic memory from the past as a target for the intervention.
2. Have the person see an image that represents the trauma in a large picture.
3. Then have the person develop a clear image of not having the trauma or being in a more resourceful, competent state. Have them place that image as a small picture in the bottom left-hand corner or the trauma picture.
4. Then have the person rapidly switch the images, so the formerly large one gets smaller and goes into the corner and the formerly small one gets large and fills the picture.

The point of these methods: shift the repetitive perceptual patterns of post-traumatic problems to resolve or dissolve the troubling aspects or eliminate them all together.

When they work, these methods seem to work almost as quickly as the neurological pattern interventions.

3.7 De-Patterning: Challenging Repetitive Patterns

As I hope you have grasped by now, there is an underlying scheme common to many successful trauma treatments, even ones not mentioned in this book or chapter; namely, they all alter the posttraumatic pattern. They usually do this via de-patterning; that is, they dissolve or challenge the repetitive patterns so the patterns cannot repeat in the same way. Recent research in brain science shows that, due to brain plasticity, the more patterns of behavior, thinking, processing, remembering, or feeling repeat, the more ingrained they become neurologically ("Neurons that fire together, wire together"). The brain, ever so adaptable, becomes more efficient at repeating these patterns the more they are repeated.

Our task, then, is to do our best to ensure that the old patterns will not repeat. This, to my mind, offers a compelling argument as to why reliving and reviving traumatic memories is not the best approach for resolving them.

Here is a list I have made up that may stimulate your thinking about where and how you can intervene in post-traumatic patterns.

Pattern Intervention Possibilities

De-patterning: Alter current patterns of action around the problem
Re-patterning: Provide alternate new patterns as substitutes for the problem

- *Change the frequency/rate of the problem or the pattern around the problem.*
- *Change the duration of the problem or the pattern around the problem.*
- *Change the time (hour/time of day, week, month or time of year) of the problem or the pattern around the problem.*
- *Change the intensity of the problem or the pattern around the problem.*
- *Change some other invariant quality of the problem or the pattern around the problem.*
- *Change the sequence (order) of events involved in or around the problem.*
- *Interrupt or otherwise prevent the occurrence of the problem.*
- *Add a new element to the problem.*
- *Break up any previously whole element of the problem into smaller elements.*
- *Have the person perform the problem without the usual accompanying pattern around it.*

- *Have the person perform the pattern around the problem at a time when they are not having the problem.*
- *Reverse the direction of striving in the performance of the problem.*
- *Link the occurrence of the problem to another pattern that is a burdensome activity.*
- *Change the body behavior/performance of the problem.*

Framing Interventions

De-framing: Challenge current frames of reference
Re-framing: Offer new frames of reference about the problem

- *Offer a new evaluation (either positive or negative) of the problem or situation.*
- *Offer a new causal explanation for the problem or situation.*
- *Use puns and humor to make new associations with the problem [Linking].*
- *Make new distinctions involving the problem [Splitting].*
- *Use analogies and anecdotes to normalize, open up new possibilities, or suggest new associations involving the problem [Linking].*
- *Orient the person's attention to some aspect of their situation or problem they haven't been attending to previously.*
- *Give their problem a new name.*
- *Externalize their problem.*

3.7.1 Find Any Regularity in the Posttraumatic Experience and Change the Pattern While the Person is Focusing on the Trauma Memory or Some Post-Trauma Problem

There are two options to create pattern changes in posttraumatic patterns: One is to have the person focus on the current problem (or "symptom") while changing some part of the neurological or perceptual aspects that have accompanied this pattern. The second is to focus on the traumatic memory itself. Either or both might work.

3.7.1.1 Neurological/Physiological Pattern Interventions

Therapist: OK, I want you to think of any aspect of the trauma or what has been haunting you about it for just a moment and pull on your earlobes. Good. Now roll your eyes all the way back in your head as far as they can go. Look at the ceiling. Now look down and to your left to the side; then down all the way to the floor on the right. Now clasp your hands and bend your fingers backwards. OK, now do you notice anything different?

Client: Well, the image is a bit more distant as I see it.

Therapist: OK. Now focus on the image again and move your tongue in your mouth in a circle. Then tip your head to one side, then the other. Notice anything else changing?

Client: Yes, the image is fading. It is getting smaller and more transparent.

Therapist: OK, good. Now, let's see if we can get it to disappear completely. Rub the back of your head, then the back of your right hand, then the back of your left hand. Tell me when the image disappears altogether.

3.7.1.2 Perceptual Pattern Intervention in the Posttraumatic Experience

Because perceptions can be part of the pattern of posttraumatic problems, we can intervene in this realm. People often report repetitive perceptions in the wake of trauma, that is, they smell something or see something from the trauma. Moreover, this

perception seems "stuck," that is, it occurs in the same way
each time it recurs. For example, I had a client who always
remembered one scene from the trauma; even though it had
lasted for some time, she was haunted by just a 30-second
piece of it. In this type of intervention, then, we are trying to
"unstick" this perceptual piece of the pattern.

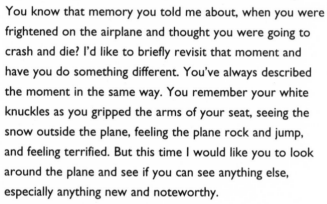

Therapist: All right. Now let's experiment with something.
You know that memory you told me about, when you were
frightened on the airplane and thought you were going to
crash and die? I'd like to briefly revisit that moment and
have you do something different. You've always described
the moment in the same way. You remember your white
knuckles as you gripped the arms of your seat, seeing the
snow outside the plane, feeling the plane rock and jump,
and feeling terrified. But this time I would like you to look
around the plane and see if you can see anything else,
especially anything new and noteworthy.

Client: Hmm, that's interesting. I see there is a woman calmly
reading a book a few rows ahead of me.

Therapist: Anything else?

Client: There is a man sleeping on my side of the plane, again
a few rows up. I can't believe he is sleeping with all that
turbulence.

Therapist: OK, now notice how you are feeling after you
noticed those other things.

Client: Well, I'm more relaxed. If those people can be so
relaxed, I guess I didn't have that much to be so frightened
about. And I did survive the plane ride.

Therapist: OK, great.

.   .   .   .

Therapist: Could you imagine the trauma scene, but see it as a
movie going backwards, and in black and white?

Client: I'll try . . . Yes, I can do that . . . That's weird. It brings a shiver to my spine. But it is interesting.

Therapist: OK, do it again, but this time run it forward and really fast.

Client: OK . . . Again, a shiver. I feel like something is letting go.

Therapist: All right. Now check back to your sense of the trauma. Anything different?

Client: Yes, I feel a little lighter about it all. Not so heavy, not so doomed.

3.7.1.3 Behavioral Pattern Intervention in the Posttraumatic Experience

This method involves getting people to shift patterns of action that repeat posttraumatically. Most people can *do* something different—action is often the most accessible aspect of the posttraumatic pattern. Of course, we usually don't ask people to make dramatic changes, but small ones.

Therapist: The next time you feel the impulse to cut yourself, I want you to take a few minutes and write down exactly what is going on in your thoughts, your body, your feelings, and anything else you can notice. Then set a timer and wait five minutes. If you still start cutting yourself, set the timer for five minutes again and stop cutting after five minutes if you haven't stopped already. Then write down a report on the same things you did before. Continue this process and find out whether this changes things.

Therapist: The next time you start to have flashbacks, if it is possible, go immediately to the bathroom, run a bath, and get into it for at least 10 minutes. Then get out, dry yourself off, and do 10 jumping jacks. Then back into the bath. I'll be interested in what happens and whether you notice any changes.

3.7.1.4   Interpersonal Pattern Intervention in the Posttraumatic Experience

Another aspect of the posttraumatic pattern is how people interact. Here we are assessing and intervening in any part of the interactional pattern surrounding or involved in the posttraumatic problem. Remember that in this approach, we are not assuming that any of these things cause the problem, only that intervening in this area might shift the pattern and dissolve the problem.

Therapist: What does your husband usually do when you are zoned out?

Client: He yells at me to come back.

Therapist: What happens for you when he does that?

Client: I feel farther away and get more zoned out.

Therapist: Your husband is a physicist, right? Tell him I'd like

him to try an experiment to see if we can get new data or a different outcome. Tell him the next time you zone out, if you do, that he should try sitting next to you, gently taking your hand, and singing a child's lullaby to you.

.   .   .   .

Client: I act badly to push everyone away. It works most of the time. Then I'm safe, but lonely.

Therapist: Would you be willing to try something new when that happens? Here's what I have in mind. It may help and it may not. The next time you feel the impulse to act badly, I would like you to write a story or draw a picture of a scared little girl who is somewhere all alone. Could you try that?

Client: OK. That might be really powerful.

3.7.1.5 Frame of Reference Pattern Intervention in the Posttraumatic Experience

Similar to the other methods in this chapter, here we are trying to shift patterns of meanings and frames of reference that have become associated with the trauma in hopes of dissolving the problem or at least helping the person begin to move a little in relation to the problem.

Client: I feel like I am the worst person in the world.

Therapist: Imagine that this trauma had happened to you daughter. What would you say to her if she were really down on herself?

Client: I would remind her that it was not her fault. And that nothing could spoil that beauty that is her soul. No matter what happened to her body, her soul was pure and good.

Therapist: Can you give any of that same message to yourself in this situation?

. . . .

Therapist: Without being glib or diminishing your pain, could you think about what possible valuable purpose this terrible experience could have served or could serve in your life?

Client: Well, one thing is that I never would have moved and met my wife if this hadn't happened to me. She's the best thing that ever happened to me and I am grateful for that.

3.7.1.6 Focus of Attention Pattern Intervention in the Posttraumatic Experience

People's attention is often riveted in the wake of trauma. This is sometimes referred to as "hypervigilance," that is, continuously scanning the environment for certain types of threats, but it can take other forms as well. Here we are searching for where the person typically focuses their attention when they are troubled and inviting them to shift their attention.

Client: I am jumpy whenever I am around men. I want to relax. I just don't feel like I can trust them.

Therapist: I think, given what happened to you, it makes sense that you might be wary of some men. The question is, "Is this man in front of me the kind of person it is appropriate to be wary of, or is he more of the trustworthy type?" I think you should pay close attention to what each man does and says and begin to really pay attention to the non-verbal and verbal signals he gives out. I'm not suggesting that you trust any men yet; just that you start to be really discerning. Pay attention to the way a particular man talks to a waiter or waitress; how he sits; how he moves or leans; how he behaves over time with people you know. Pay particular attention to his eyes and his mouth and tell me what you are learning and discovering next time you are here.

. . . .

Therapist: The next time you start having flashbacks, I want you to touch anything around you in the real world, especially anything with a texture. Find something that is rough or smooth or bumpy or soft. Just keep touching it to ground you in this reality and bring you back from flashback-land.

3.7.1.7 Location Pattern Intervention in the Posttraumatic Experience

Here we are suggesting that people try changing their physical location when they experience the posttraumatic problem as a way of getting unstuck. In order to do this, find any regularity of where people are when they are experiencing the posttraumatic problem and suggest they change locations. The change could be within their house or office or it could be outside.

Therapist: When you start to feel disconnected and dissociated, I suggest you take a walk in the nearest park.
Client: What good would that do?
Therapist: Well, I am operating on the idea that we get stuck sometimes in the wake of trauma and that changing scenes might help get you unstuck. The other aspect is that being in nature is sometimes healing for people, according to some research.
Client: Okay, I'll give it a try, but I don't know how much good it will do.
Therapist: It's just an experiment. It might work and it might not. But it's worth a try, since you told me nothing else is helping yet.

A variation on this method of changing locations is to move the posttraumatic pattern outside the person's body. I call this *externalizing*.

Let me illustrate this concept further. I had a client who had been cutting herself. We had an agreement that she would not cut herself while in treatment with me. But at one point during treatment, she told me she wasn't sure she could keep the agreement, as the impulse to cut was becoming more urgent and overwhelming.

I found an antique Raggedy Ann doll that happened to be the same age she was and gave it to her. I suggested she cut the doll instead of herself. She was able to do this. She also sewed the doll up after cutting it, and this turned out to be very healing for her. She cried while she was sewing the doll and reported that she had connected with some deep grief she had never allowed herself to feel fully.

You might be able to present this method to your client by saying something like this:

Therapist: I'd like you to find something physical that represents the trauma you have been carrying around. Carry that thing around with you for the next week and then find someplace appropriate and meaningful to get rid of that object.

The idea in externalizing is to change the location of the problem from inside the person to outside.

3.7.1.8 Environment Pattern Intervention in the Posttraumatic Experience

This is a slight variation on the last method. Instead of just shifting location, we are thinking about environment here and suggesting a change in that part of the pattern.

Therapist: The next time you become frightened, if it is possible, I would like you to go spend time in the most sacred place you know and can get to. Try this and let me

know what happens. I think it might create a helpful shift of
some kind.

Client: I know exactly where I will go. There is this meditation
space in my building, with a wall of plants. It is very peaceful
and holy in there. I'll give it a try.

.   .   .   .

Therapist: Now you two have told me
that when you begin to have sex,
sometimes she gets frightened and
regresses back to her abuse. I have
a suggestion that might work. You
mentioned that you have sex in the dark.
If she begins to regress, I suggest you turn on the
light and have her feel your face until she knows it is you
and not her abuser. Then continue if you both feel OK
about it.

There is a second way to change the pattern, called *re-patterning*,
that is, offering a new pattern, more functional and less painful,
in place of the old one. In a sense, we are re-grooving the brain.
We'll take that up in the next section.

3.8 Solution-Oriented Methods

I mentioned in the introduction that I was strongly influenced
by Milton Erickson's "resource" orientation to therapy. He
saw people as having resources, abilities and strengths—some
inherent and some developed through life experiences—that
could be used to resolve their problems. I think that people
who have experienced trauma often have strengths that allowed
them to survive and get through those challenging experiences,
and they also often develop abilities and coping mechanisms as a
result of the trauma.

For some years, I worked at developing an approach to change that involved investigating, highlighting, and evoking what worked in people's lives as a solution to the problems that were troubling them. This can also be helpful in changing the posttraumatic pattern in two ways: One is that we can find what worked to help, diminish, or solve the problem previously; and two, we can find a pattern that can substitute for the unhelpful posttraumatic pattern.

3.8.1 Investigating and Substituting Solution Patterns

As troubled as people can be in the wake of trauma, they also often have resources. One of those resources is knowledge and experience using patterns that work. Here we investigate their solution patterns, that is, the things they do that work, and suggest they substitute those patterns for the problem ones when they can.

Therapist: You mentioned you have been drinking to excess many nights. Tell me about a night when you either didn't drink or didn't drink to excess.

Client: Well, when I am busy with something that interests me, I don't drink or at least don't drink much.

Therapist: Like what?

Client: If I have a friend over. Or if I am working on my art. Or if I can get involved in a really good book.

Therapist: OK, let's see if we can use any of those deliberately to help diminish this troublesome drinking.

.   .   .   .

Therapist: You mentioned that years ago, you had forgiven someone who had done something terrible to you. How did you let that go and move on?

Client: Well, I had recently had an insight while at my church. Something that was said during the minister's sermon made me realize that Jesus had died on the cross so we could all be forgiven for our sins. The minister then said that if we forgive others, we can be forgiven ourselves, but if we don't, we have no room in our heart for Jesus's forgiveness. All at once, I felt a total letting go of all my resentment.

Therapist: Do you think you could use a similar process to let go of this trauma?

Client: I never thought of that. Maybe.

In Chapter One, I offered a dollop of theory in regards to trauma. I mentioned the "frozen in time" aspect of trauma; that is, in the aftereffects of trauma, an aspect of the person seems to stay frozen in the past, in the traumatic moment. That moment loops and repeats itself in the present when triggered by some association, or it just becomes a regular presence in the person's life, constantly replaying and looping even when not triggered.

In this chapter, we have discussed some methods for breaking up this repetitive loop by breaking the pattern, almost like smashing ice into pieces. In the next chapter, I will detail another method for dissolving the posttraumatic pattern: reconnection.

Reconnection: Challenging Dissociation and Disconnection in the Wake of Trauma

One of the key characteristics central to most, if not all, posttraumatic issues is dissociation or disconnection. Trauma survivors have been known to disconnect from their general sense of themselves—that is, they understand mentally that things are happening to them, but they can't directly and deeply experience or feel those things. This is sometimes called "depersonalization." There have been reports of people disconnecting from their bodies. One of my clients told me she was frequently bruised because she often ran into the furniture; she was so dissociated from her body in the aftermath of her trauma that she barely noticed it, or noticed when she was about to walk into something and injure her body.

Think of a dog that gets hit by a car on the road. The dog is lying in a ditch when you approach it to see if it is OK or needs to be taken to a veterinarian. What happens when you approach the dog? It growls or snaps at you to keep you away. It has been hurt and it is trying to protect itself. If you actually get close enough to touch the dog to examine it, it will shrink away from your touch.

The natural response to trauma is to push away or withdraw from those around us, even those offering help. People disconnect from aspects of themselves when they are overwhelmed by feelings, sensations, and experiences that they simply cannot process or understand. They avoid others by pulling away because they feel alienated from them or frightened of how they might act in front of, or be perceived by, them. This is a protective reaction and makes sense. But when the disconnection continues on for too long after the trauma, it can become troubling and turn into "symptoms" that lead a person to seek therapy.

In this chapter, then, we will take up another way to assist people with rapid recovery from trauma aftereffects: helping them reconnect where they have become disconnected.

4.1 Seven Pathways to Connection

I have divided the ways in which and places where people can get disconnected and reconnected into three categories and seven areas. The three categories are:

1. Personal: We examine the ways people can get disconnected from themselves (that is, one's deep self or inner self, or one's body) and ways to reconnect them internally.
2. Interpersonal: We examine the ways people grow alienated and disconnected socially, whether from their intimates or from their communities, and how to reconnect them in those areas.
3. Transpersonal: We examine the ways in which people become disconnected from the things that call them beyond themselves and beyond the realm of humankind (such as nature, art, and religion) and how to help them get more connected in those areas.

The next sections will detail each of these three types of disconnection, and some methods that can be used to facilitate reconnection.

4.1.1 The Deep Self/Inner Self Disconnection/Reconnection

In the wake of trauma, people sometimes disconnect from themselves, their feelings, and their own inner knowledge. They leave themselves—and in some cases, they don't fully return over time. Treatment can help identify these kinds of self-disconnections and help the person make a reconnection to their self.

I had a client who told me she never really knew her reaction to a situation, whether she was sad, happy, angry, scared, or anything else emotional. When she was a child, this knowledge had been overwhelming, given the traumas she routinely suffered. As an adult, several days after a significant event, she would finally come to realize how she had been feeling during that event.

During treatment, she came up with this plan to address her emotional disconnection. Every night she would lock the door to her house and then the one to her bedroom so she would feel safe. Then she would put on some soothing music, light some incense, and drink some relaxing tea while writing in her journal. She would write about the day's significant event and try to work out what she might have been feeling during or in reaction to it.

In one session, she triumphantly announced that she had felt her feelings about a particular situation only four hours after it happened. By the end of treatment, she was (mostly) feeling her feelings right when they occurred. This is what I mean by reconnecting to one's inner or deeper self.

In this section we are inviting people to reconnect, whether by discovering their natural, but perhaps recently unused ways of doing so, or by suggesting ways to reconnect that might work.

Therapist: How do you get in touch with what is going on with you?
Client: I used to meditate, but I haven't done that for a long time. It was nice, though. I would go to this calm center and thoughts and feelings would just bubble up. Maybe I should take it up again.
Therapist: From what you tell me, that might be a good idea. Since you make these unfortunate relationship choices, maybe knowing what is going on with you would help you avoid some mistakes.

· · · · · · · · · · · · · · · · ·

Client: I can't remember anything from about fourth grade on.
Therapist: Can you bring in some pictures from those blank years next session and just talk me through them?

· · · · · · · · · · · · · · · ·

Client: I almost never cry. It's like I'm numb.
Therapist: You said, "almost never." When do you or have you cried?
Client: When I watch a movie in which someone is unexpectedly kind to someone who needs kindness. I'm a softie. My wife kids me about it.
Therapist: And what do you suppose moves you about those kinds of scenes?

Client: I've never thought about it . . . I guess I longed for that when I was young. And rarely got it. [Begins to tear up.]

. . . .

Client: I have this weird thing that happens all the time. I don't experience the world directly. It is like I am seeing my past on a screen in front of me, and that screen is between me and everyone and everything that happens.

Therapist: Could you try making another screen? This one would have your current experience on one screen and the past on another.

Client: Yeah, I could try. OK, I am making another screen. I guess I'm good at the screen thing. It's there now.

Therapist: OK, now, could you just stay with the two screens? Find out whether you can connect the things that are happening on the present screen with the things that are happening on the past screen.

Things that might help people connect to themselves and their deeper realities and sensibilities include:

- Meditating
- Journaling
- Taking walks alone
- Spending silent time
- Reading
- Guided imagery
- Self-help books

4.1.2 The Body Disconnection/Reconnection

In this section, we'll explore ways to assess any disconnection trauma survivors might be experiencing from their physical bodies or bodily experiences, and help them reconnect.

In this aspect of inviting or exploring reconnection, we will
focus on physical/bodily reconnection. Because so many
people experience trauma through the body, it is very
common to find people dissociated from their sensory, bodily
experience.

Client: I am addicted to Internet porn. I'm spending way too
much money and time on it. I think it's going to wreck my
marriage and maybe my whole life.

Therapist: And you have a sense that this is related to your
sexual trauma?

Client: Yes. I am not gay but I find myself sneaking these looks
at gay porn sites. I'm disgusted with myself afterward. I
don't get aroused. It's like some weird and unsatisfying
compulsion. I think, since I was abused by a male, I am
trying to prove to myself that I am not gay. Why can't I
stop this?

Therapist: OK, let's have you try something different next
time you get this compulsion. Set a timer and spend five
minutes just checking in with your body and note what is
happening.

[Next session]

Client: I tried the experiment several times. Each time I felt
these butterflies in my stomach. I stayed with that sensation
for longer than five minutes. I vowed to myself I would
get to the bottom of this. The second time, the butterflies
changed to anger and I stayed with that. It was a burning in
my stomach and a fire in my heart. Then that sort of burned
itself out and I sobbed more deeply than I have in years. The
interesting thing is that after that cry, I felt settled. I haven't
looked at porn since then. I'm not sure the compulsion is
completely gone, but I feel less frantic and out of control.

Things that might help people connect to their bodies
include:

- Exercising
- Relaxation training
- Slow and mindful eating
- Sensory awareness training
- Safe and pleasurable sex
- Massage

4.1.3 Another Being Disconnection/ Reconnection

I used to have another name for this one—Another Person
Disconnection/Reconnection—until I had a client who told
me that her only connection was with her beloved pet
dog. She felt alienated from people and was profoundly
dissociated from herself. So, I changed it to "being"
instead of person, to be inclusive of bonds with non-
human living things.

In this section, we are searching for any connections and
disconnections in the area of one-to-one relationships, whether
they be human or animal.

Therapist: Is there anyone with whom you have a close,
trusting relationship?
Client: No, no one.
Therapist: Not even a pet?
Client: Oh, I thought you meant people. I love my cat.
Sometimes I wish all people would disappear. I like animals
much better than people.

Client: I want to kill myself. I have for years.

Therapist: And how have you stopped yourself from acting on that impulse?

Client: My daughter. I could never leave her with that legacy. I have read that children whose parents kill themselves are much more likely to kill themselves too. I love her too much to do that to her.

Therapist: So, you have kept yourself going through a lot of misery in large part due to that love. And that is in part what brought you here to try to reduce or eliminate that pain?

Client: Yeah, I guess so. I'm not sure I believe that it can change, though.

Here are some simple suggestions for connecting with one other person or being in the wake of trauma to help the healing:

- Get a pet
- Take up horse riding
- Volunteer to help someone less fortunate than you
- Re-connect with an old friend with whom you have lost contact

Obviously, these won't always work and one must be careful not to impose these on people.

4.1.4 Community/Groups Disconnection/Reconnection

In this section, we check where the person is alienated from his or her fellow humans in general, and if and where they could connect or re-connect with a sense of being in community.

As I was writing this chapter, I came across some relevant research. Researchers investigating the aftereffects of a devastating earthquake discovered that survivors who were with others during the ordeal suffered less post-traumatic effects than those who were alone (Armenian et. al, 2000). Maryann Burns, a Cantor Fitzgerald employee who missed her train the morning of 9/11 and thus was not killed (as were hundred of her fellow employees, since their office was at the top of the World Trade Center) said the following five years after the attack, on the subject of working at her re-constituted company, where there were many others like her who had survived: "The only place I felt like myself was work. I needed to be around other people who'd been where I'd been. I didn't want to have to explain myself. In groups of other people I often felt detached, you know? Distracted. Work made me feel sane. I wanted to go to work every day. I still do" (http://www.businessweek.com/magazine/content/06_37/b4000077.htm).

We can use this idea of connecting with others to help people heal from trauma.

Therapist: Is there some place or group where you feel comfortable, like you belong?

Client: Yeah. I skateboard and those people feel like my real family. I spend a lot of time with them.

Therapist: What gives you a sense of belonging with them?

Client: They don't judge you. Most of us are outcasts. We aren't the popular kids. So there is a lot of acceptance. Most of them are really smart too. I like that. I'm smart and don't like to pretend to be dumb just to fit in.

Therapist: Do you think finding that kind of acceptance has helped you heal from your trauma in any way?

Client: I never considered it, but maybe so in a way.

. . . .

Client: I don't feel like I fit anywhere.

Therapist: Have you ever felt like you fit somewhere in the past?

Client: I belonged to a church when I lived in California. They had great music and the pastor was really hip. He was like a real person, you know.

Therapist: Have you tried to find a similar kind of church here?

Client: No, I kind of figured I wouldn't find anything like that and I would be disappointed.

Therapist: Maybe so, but I suggest you look around. Maybe you'll find something that fits. You are pretty isolated.

Client: Yeah, I am. OK, I'll give it a try.

Things that might help people connect to groups and communities include:

- Joining a religious congregation
- Volunteering for group charity activities
- Joining a support group
- Participating in professional associations
- Family get-togethers and reunions
- Work groups
- Participating in advocacy and community groups

4.1.5 Nature Disconnection/Reconnection

There is some evidence of a connection with nature being healing (see Burns, 1998; Frumkin, 2001). In this section, we will investigate where people are disconnected from nature and how to help them get reconnected, or connected for the first time, as part of their healing.

Like connecting to social groups, I suspect this connection to nature has to do with our evolution. We evolved both in groups, in tribes, and in natural settings. So perhaps it is wired into us to be connected to nature, to notice our natural surroundings, to feel connected with them. If we are alienated from them, we might feel a bit unsettled. Regardless of the reasons for this, I and others have discovered that helping people connect to nature can be helpful. The following dialogues show some ways this might be done in a clinical setting.

Therapist: Is there someplace you go in nature to renew yourself or heal?

Client: No, I prefer indoor sports. I am on the computer most of the time.

Therapist: I have an experiment I'd like you to try. When the weather is good one day soon, bring your computer outside. Find someplace beautiful and just set up there.

Client: I'd need an Internet connection. That wouldn't work.

Therapist: Oh, OK. I have a portable Internet service I can use anywhere, so I didn't think of that. Well, either you could find some beautiful spot that has access to public Wi-Fi, or you could actually try going computer-free for a half an hour or so, and just try out some nature time. The reason I suggest this is that some people believe that being in nature can help heal trauma.

Client: I never heard of that. I'll think about it. My friends say I'm like a vampire and never get any sun. I guess it couldn't hurt to give it a try.

Sometimes, you can simply encourage your client to remember a pleasant or meaningful experience that took place in a natural setting. This can be enough to reap the healing benefits of the natural world.

Client: The best moment in my life was on a beach in Mexico. I was there with friends, playing music and dancing naked. I felt absolutely spiritual and whole.

Therapist: Can you get some of that feeling back while you focus on the things you need to overcome right now?

Things that might help people connect to nature include:

- Walking outside
- Visiting the ocean or forest
- Visiting national parks
- Bicycle riding
- Creating a view of nature at work

4.1.6 Art Disconnection/Reconnection

It is not simply a coincidence that many trauma survivors use art to reconnect with themselves, or even to leave their trauma behind. I heard a story about Bob Simon, a reporter who was taken captive by the Iraqis during the first Gulf War. He was Jewish and feared for his life during his captivity. After he was released he wrote a book about his ordeal. When asked if reading the book after writing it brought up posttraumatic feelings, he said that once he wrote the book, he felt that the trauma was now contained in the book and he was essentially over it.

Trauma survivors sometimes report that they connect through reading someone else's account of trauma, or they feel healed after they hear music that captures a feeling they have never been able to articulate or fully feel, or they see a painting and it helps them transcend their suffering and feel something profound. These reports point to the possibility that we can help people connect or reconnect through viewing someone else's art or by creating their own art.

Therapist: Do you make any art or music? Or do you write?
Client: I wrote poetry.
Therapist: Do you think that writing helps you heal?
Client: Yes, it's definitely part of the healing.
Therapist: Can you write some poetry between now and the next session and bring it in here for me to get a sense of things beyond our conversation here? Sometimes art brings out things that can't be said in normal, everyday conversations.
Client: That would be really cool. Sure.

. . . .

Client: I saw this movie that was really weird, but in some ways I think it helped me. It was called El Topo.
Therapist: How did it help you?
Client: It is hard to say. It was really powerful visually and I felt something shift inside me while I was watching it. The friend I was with thought it was horrible, but I just felt like these broken pieces of me were just getting repaired or glued back together the whole time the film was unreeling. I don't want to see it again. I'm afraid that seeing it a second time might undo something or I would start to intellectualize it or something.
Therapist: It sounds like there was something very powerful in that experience. And if I were you, I would trust that sense of not seeing it again. Just remembering that healing and that such integration is possible is enough.

Things that might help people connect to art include creating or participating in:

- Reading
- Painting
- Dancing
- Writing
- Sculpting
- Pottery
- Movies
- Music

4.1.7 Disconnection from and Reconnection with a Greater Meaning, Purpose, God, or a Higher Power

There are some who believe that trauma has such a devastating effect because it shatters meaning. I have had clients tell me that they thought God was punishing them through their traumatic experience, or that they felt, in the aftermath of their trauma, that God had let them down. Sometimes a trauma causes a person to lose their faith or belief in God or a higher power of some kind. So, sometimes the greater meaning of life can get lost for people who have experienced overwhelming trauma. Part of our work, as therapists, can be to help them reconnect with or restore that meaning to their own lives.

One must be careful in this area. Some people have been so traumatized or shamed in their experience of religion that they have a negative reaction to any religious terms. Still others find these terms extremely meaningful and important, so not using them could be alienating for them. As always, let the client and your clinical (and human) sensitivity guide you and make mid-course corrections after any missteps.

Client: I think God had it out for me. I used to be really religious but He let me down.

Therapist: How so?

Client: I was a good Christian. And then He let this shit happen to me.

Therapist: Have you spoken with your old pastor about it?

Client: No. I guess I never gave him a chance. I thought he'd just feed me some line about how God's ways are a mystery and we don't understand why these things happen. I didn't need that bullshit.

Therapist: Is that the kind of pastor he was?

Client: No, he actually wasn't. He was no bullshit. I guess I was just really mad at God. Maybe I could go talk to the pastor. It might help. My religion was really important to me. I'm sorry I lost it.

. . . .

Therapist: You've told me that you feel you lost the thread of your life after the murder. Tell me how you think about the course of your life and where you are in it now, after some time has passed.

Client: Yeah, I felt like I didn't know who I was anymore and what life meant. Or whether life had any meaning. I would watch people go about their lives and I felt like they were in some sort of delusional bubble. They didn't know it was all an illusion.

Therapist: And has anything changed since those days?

Client: Yes, I think so. I mean now that I have some distance from the event, I can start to see that life does have some meaning. The laugh of a child, which was like burning coals to me before, now sounds sweet. That is the meaning of life. To have a moment of love, of sweetness, of laughter, with someone you care about. Or just to feel the sun on your face after a long winter. Yes, I think I'm starting to come

back to life and find my place in it. It doesn't seem like the
sham it did.

Things that might help people connect to bigger meaning
include:

* Joining a religious congregation
* Volunteering

* Writing about one's traumatic experiences
* Starting a charitable foundation related to one's trauma
* Reading spiritual material
* Finding the meaning in one's suffering
* Finding one's life purpose

4.2 Connective and Stability Rituals

Another way to help people connect is to help them find or
reestablish what I call "connective rituals." These are rituals, or
regularly repeated activities that help people connect in any of
the three areas of connection and disconnection detailed above
(personal, interpersonal, and transpersonal).

I met the woman known for years only as the Central Park
Jogger; in 1989, she had been brutally attacked in the park and
left for dead. She miraculously recovered over the course of
many years, and wanted to renew her habit of running, which
had been a great joy to her, as well as a pleasing fitness routine.
She liked to run in Central Park, but after that attack, it didn't
seem safe to do so. She started running on a treadmill, but
found it less satisfying, since it didn't allow her to be outside, in
nature.

She eventually found a neighbor and friend, a former Marine,
who was willing to go running through Central Park with her. In

this way, she was able to restore a ritual that had been missing from her life and helped, in some part, to heal her.

In this part of reconnecting, we are helping people discover new or restore previous rituals, perhaps altering those old rituals in a way that updates them to take current realities into account.

Client: I haven't been able to have sex with my husband since that took place. It is putting a strain on our relationship. He and I both feel disconnected.

Therapist: Could you find some less intense and challenging ways to reconnect physically? Like giving massages? Or bathing each other tenderly?

Client: I never thought of that. I like getting massages and he likes giving them. If I could get him to promise not to turn them into a sexual encounter, we could try that.

. . . .

Therapist: Can you think of some daily activity that you could establish that would help give you some sense of connection to your body?

Client: I'd like to walk daily. Walking is like a massage for my mind. It relaxes me. My thoughts just wander and I really enjoy that.

Therapist: OK. What will it take for you to do that and keep the habit going?

Client: Just talking to my family and letting them know that I am starting this and I won't be available for an hour or so each evening.

4.3 The Writing Cure

There are two books that summarize a simple method that has been shown to be remarkably effective at helping people quickly move on from trauma. They are *Opening Up: The Healing Power of Expressing Emotions,* by James Pennebaker, and *The Writing Cure: How Expressive Writing Promotes Health and Emotional Well-Being,* edited by Stephen J. Lepore and Joshua M. Smyth. These books summarize a large amount of research that has been replicated many times and with different types of traumas. The research consistently shows the positive effects of writing about trauma and crisis.

What surprised me about this research is that people only have to write for as little as 15 minutes a day, for as few as four or five days. This writing has been show to be correlated with:

- Far fewer visits to the student health center for college students
- Reduced absenteeism at work
- Fewer medical visits for breast cancer patients
- An increase in T-cells (immune system functioning)
- Healthier liver enzyme (from reduced alcohol consumption)
- Less pain for arthritis patients
- Better lung functioning for asthma patients
- Increased likelihood and rapidity of getting a new job after being laid off
- Reduced anxiety and depression
- Improved grades
- Improved mental and physical health of grade-school students, people in nursing homes, arthritis patients, medical students, rape victims, new mothers, and prisoners.

However, the writing must be done in some pretty specific ways in order to get the maximum benefit. Here are the instructions I give people based on this research.

Guidelines for Writing Your Way Out of Trauma

1. Write honestly and openly about your deepest feelings and thoughts concerning the situation you are in or went through. Make sure you keep these writings private, or you may find yourself unconsciously censoring what you write and diluting the effects of the writing.

2. Write for a relatively short time, say 15 to 30 minutes. This writing is often draining or emotionally difficult. Limiting the time makes it both a bit more tolerable and more likely that you will do it.

3. Write for only four or five days. You can write occasionally over the course of several weeks, or write four or five days in a row. This time limit seemed to work very well in the experiments that were done. They are not carved in stone, however, and if you find you need more time, you can take it. One of the points of this limit of a few days is, again, to contain the experience so it doesn't take over your life or drop you back into the trauma.

4. Try to find both a private and unique place to write, somewhere you can be uninterrupted and someplace that isn't associated with other things or that has the usual smells, sights, and sounds of places you already know well.

5. Don't worry about grammar or spelling or getting it right. Just write.

6. On the days you do write, try to write at the same time each day. It's not crucial, but it can sometimes give your unconscious mind some structure and preparation time if it knows exactly when the writing will take place. This can also help contain the emotions and intrusive thinking that may occur and interfere with your day or evening.

7. Writing seems to be the most powerful mode of expression, but if for some reason that won't work for you, you could try "writing" by speaking into a tape recorder or a video camera.

8. You don't have to "be positive," but if you can, include in your writing some of the benefits that have occurred or positive things you have gotten out of your crisis, like becoming closer to someone, or exercising more, for example.

9. *After the writing times are done, consider burning the pages you have written. This gives some people closure and a sense of leaving the trauma behind.*

10. *Ignore these guidelines if you discover something else that works better for you. Everyone is unique.*

4.4 Transition and Disconnective Rituals for Moving on from Trauma

Another kind of ritual is almost the opposite of connective rituals: This kind helps people leave old traumas behind by performing a ritual of letting go or leaving. For this kind of ritual, which is usually a one-time thing, the person usually needs to find a physical object that symbolizes the trauma or some unfinished issues. The symbolic object is then carried around for a period of time, so it really becomes imbued with the feelings or unfinished emotions or issues. Then, the person is encouraged to throw the symbolic object away, burn it, bury it, or leave it someplace meaningful.

Client: I just want to forget all this and move on.

Therapist: I have an idea. Could you find something that represents your father? Some object that reminds you of him or belonged to him?

Client: I have some things of his that I took from the house after he died. I have some shoes of his that aren't my size and I will never wear. I don't even know why I have kept them all this time. Maybe for this kind of thing. Maybe my subconscious knew that I would need to do something with them sometime.

Therapist: OK, I suggest you carry those shoes around with you everywhere for the next week and then find some significant and meaningful place to leave them.

Client: I could leave them at his grave. I've never visited it. There are some things I would like to say to him out there.

Therapist: Good. Is there some significant date coming up any time soon?

Client: My mother's birthday is two weeks from yesterday.

Therapist: If that would work, leave the shoes at the grave and have that talk on that day.

Therapist: Can you think of something you could do with the piece of the car wreckage you still have that would symbolize moving on and putting this behind you?

Client: Yeah, I could go back to the scene of the accident and leave it there. It really belongs there. I shouldn't keep it in my life.

Now we have covered the four rapid methods of resolving trauma, but we're not done yet. We will now add one more piece: the notion that traumatic aftereffects aren't uniformly negative. In the next chapter, we'll take up and explore the notion that, sometimes, positive developments can happen in the wake of terrible tragedies.

Posttraumatic Success: Thriving Through Crisis

(5)

So far in this book, we have been discussing ways to rapidly resolve trauma. In this chapter, we'll go further than that, by delving into the evidence for and means of turning trauma into growth and positive change.

5.1 Posttraumatic Growth Inventory and Methods

Psychologist Richard Tedeschi and colleagues developed the Posttraumatic Growth Inventory, an instrument for assessing positive outcomes reported by persons who have experienced traumatic events. This 21-item scale includes factors such as New Possibilities, Relating to Others, Personal Strength, Spiritual Change, and Appreciation of Life (you or your clients can access this scale for no charge at http://cust-cf.apa.org/ptgi/). I'll note here that this research goes beyond the notion of "resilience," in which people bounce back from traumatic events. These people report positive changes directly or indirectly coming from having gone through traumatic events.

Here are some sample statements from the Posttraumatic Growth Inventory. People taking the inventory are to rate each item on a scale of 1 to 5, in terms of how little (1) to how much (5) the trauma or crisis led to developments such as:

I established a new path for my life.
I know better that I can handle difficulties.

I changed my priorities about what is important in life.

New opportunities are available which wouldn't have been
   otherwise.

I have more compassion for others.

I discovered that I'm stronger than I thought I was.

I have a greater sense of closeness with others.

Using the Posttraumatic Growth Inventory, Tedeschi and others
have discovered that women tend to report more benefits than
men do and people who have experienced traumatic events
report more positive change than do people who have not
experienced them.

Another scale, developed independently and measuring slightly
different things after tragic life events, is the Perceived Benefits
of Adversity Scale. This measurement tool found positive posttraumatic changes in eight areas:

- Lifestyle changes
- Material gain
- Increases in self efficacy
- Increases in family closeness
- Increases in community closeness
- Increase in faith in people
- Increase in compassion
- Increase in spirituality

You can find out more in the literature in this area, but suffice
it to say that our notions of post-traumatic experience have
shifted as a result of this work (Linley & Joseph, 2004).

Now, you must be very careful not to put words in the mouths
of clients, and not to be insensitive to their suffering by being
too positive. It can be a delicate balancing act, because we don't

want to ignore positive developments either. So, use your clinical skills and sensitivity to stay connected to people when you are using the methods in this chapter, and you should be fine.

Of course, many people will have had mixed experiences, some negative and some positive, in the wake of trauma. The best thing to do is to investigate it all, stay open, listen, and respond empathically, without closing down possibilities or imposing any meanings or conclusions one way or the other. You task is to investigate and highlight any positive changes in the wake of trauma, without minimizing the suffering or tragedy involved.

5.1.1 Investigate or Highlight Any Positive Developments that Arose from the Trauma

One must be careful here not to be glib or imposing, but also not to ignore or not investigate any positive developments that arose from the traumatic event.

Most people will have a mixture of good and bad, in my experience. But in psychotherapy, we are often so focused on the negative aspects (after all, that is probably what brought people to treatment), that we sometimes give short shrift to any growth or positive elements in the wake of trauma.

Therapist: A certain percentage of people who go through terrible experiences say that, even though the experience was awful, something surprisingly good came from it. Have you noticed anything like that?

Client: I find I cry more since I went through that.

Therapist: Is that a good thing or not?

Client: Oh, it's definitely a good thing. I think I was a little closed off before, but now I am more sensitive to my own feelings as well as the suffering of others.

5.1.2 Investigate and Inquire about Positive Relationship Changes in the Aftermath of the Trauma

One of the most common reports of positive experience after trauma is a shift in relationships. Some people report an increased appreciation of others; others report a newfound compassion or kindness for others; still others report an increase in their expression of affection and love for others. These dialogues will illustrate how you might go about discovering any of these positive changes.

Therapist: Have you gotten closer to anyone in your life as a result of going through this trauma?
Client: I appreciate my kids more. I do less yelling and more listening. I realize that every moment with them is precious, so I don't want to spoil it or waste it.

Therapist: Sometimes these newfound appreciations and changes fade over time as we get more distance from the dramatic events that brought them about. Can you think of a way to keep these positive developments going?
Client: Well, I have a chunk of the twisted metal from the wreck. I could take it out every once in a while and contemplate "what might have been." That will probably help me remember.

. . . .

Therapist: How has going through all this changed your relationships, for the better or worse?
Client: Well, my wife says that I am more open with her.
Therapist: How so?

Client: She says I tell her what I am thinking more
and make sure to tell her when to expect
me home.

Therapist: Do you agree that you are more
open with her? And is that a good thing?

Client: Yeah, I think so. She is much more affectionate
with me, I've noticed. And I like that. So, it's a good thing.

Therapist: Any other relationships change, have you noticed?

Client: I am more compassionate with everyone. I read this
interview with Bob Dylan. He said his grandmother used to
tell him: Be kind, for everyone you meet is fighting a hard
battle.

5.1.3 Investigate or Highlight any Newfound Knowledge or Development of Strengths that Emerged from the Trauma

People also report that they have discovered or developed
strengths in the wake of trying experiences. Here, we will
investigate whether the client has had any of those positive
developments.

Therapist: Have you recognized or developed any strengths
now that you have come through the trauma?

. . . .

Therapist: Do you find you can handle challenging things better
since emerging from this terrible time?

5.1.4 Investigate or Highlight New Directions or Possibilities that Have Opened Up for the Person in Relation to the Trauma

This is a more generic investigation of any positive
developments that have arisen because of or since the tragedy

occurred. Here we are focused on new possibilities that have
opened up.

Therapist: Have you changed your life course in any way
    due to the trauma? Has the trauma opened up any new
    possibilities that weren't there before you went through it?
Client: I stood up to a bully at work. He was browbeating a
    secretary and I told him to back off.
Therapist: Was that something you would have done before
    you were raped?
Client: No. I probably would have just slinked away and decided
    it was none of my business. But since I was raped, I just
    can't take bullies, especially men bullying women.
Therapist: So, you consider this a good change?
Client: Yes. I feel stronger and like I have more integrity
    somehow; that I am truer to myself these days. I don't hide
    who I am or what I feel as much.
Therapist: And do you have a sense that this change is
    permanent or will carry on?
Client: I'm not sure. I want it to.

5.1.5 Investigate or Highlight How the Person's Appreciation of Life Has Changed for the Better Since the Trauma

Sometimes people are grateful just to be alive after surviving
a trauma. Or they stop taking everyday life for granted. Here
we explore this area to find out whether the person has
experienced either of these positive developments.

Client: I wake up every morning and feel grateful to be alive,
    you know. I mean, I could easily be dead and here it is,
    another sunrise.

Therapist: I guess we could all use a bit more of
that sense. Can you say more about that?
What would you say to someone who takes
life for granted?
Client: Well, I would tell them you have to
realize that life is fragile. Any one of us could die
at any moment. And that life itself is a precious thing. If
you've ever lost a loved one or a beloved pet, you know
how precious it is and you would sometimes give anything
to have a bit more time with that person or the pet. That's
the way it can be with your own life—just this sense of
being grateful for every hour, every day, every minute.

5.1.6 Investigate or Highlight Positive Spiritual Changes or Realizations that Have Come About Since the Trauma

People who weren't previously religious or spiritual sometimes
find a newfound faith or spiritual life in the wake of trauma. In
these snippets of dialogue, you might get some ideas about how
to gently explore this area.

Client: I started meditating again.
Therapist: What got you to do that?
Client: I think I need to be able to be more calm and trusting. I
have been more on edge since she had the affair. I used to
be able to be calm and give things up to a higher power, but
now I find myself obsessing and monitoring her every mood.
That drives her away and makes me crazy. Meditating is
a way of both calming down and getting in touch with my
soul and something bigger than me that I can trust. It helps
me feel like the universe is friendly and gets my mind off
negative things.

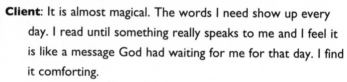

Therapist: Have you noticed any shifts in you spiritual or religious life since the trauma?

Client: Yes, I think so. I read the Bible more regularly and find it helpful.

Therapist: What do you find helpful about reading the Bible more regularly?

Client: It is almost magical. The words I need show up every day. I read until something really speaks to me and I feel it is like a message God had waiting for me for that day. I find it comforting.

Therapist: Have you found yourself being more spiritual after this terrible experience?

Client: Yes, I feel like I am here for a purpose. My purpose is to help stop animal cruelty. I have always had a soft spot for animals, but now, since I have had this trauma, I can't stand that animals are suffering in any way. They can't speak up or defend themselves, so we humans have to be their protectors. I feel like this is the reason I went through that trauma and like I have found some direction for my energy outside of work. It feels like a sacred duty to help the animals.

5.2 The 3 C's of Posttraumatic Success

My own idea about posttraumatic success is built on the 3 C's: Connection (which we have discussed in Chapter Four), Compassion, and Contribution.

I have found, both in my clinical and life experience and in reading the literature, that people who stay disconnected in

the wake of the trauma, who have diminished compassion
(or more judgmental harshness or meanness), and who have
withdrawn from their sense of contributing to the betterment
of others and the world suffer more posttraumatic symptoms.
The opposite holds as well: Those who connect more deeply
to themselves, others, and something beyond themselves, those
who develop a stronger or deeper compassion for others,
and those who contribute to something that makes the world
or other people better in the wake of trauma have fewer
posttraumatic symptoms and troubles and even thrive and grow.

In this section, then, I will detail some methods that derive from
these three C's.

5.2.1 Investigating Stronger Connections in the Wake of Trauma

This section harkens back to the previous chapter on
connections and disconnections, but here we are investigating
spontaneously strengthened connections that have arisen in the
wake of trauma, in part to highlight them for the person and in
part to discover potential sources of strength and pathways to
healing for anything that might still be troubling people.

Therapist: There is a Hemingway line that talks about being
"strong in the broken places." Is there any place you think
you have become stronger as a result of the trauma you
went through?

Client: I think I am closer to my sister because
of it. She was really there for me. Before,
we had a stormy relationship because
we fought so much as kids and we
were always competing for my father's
affection. But now we're solid. It seems strange,

but going through this suicidal depression created the best relationship we have ever had.

Therapist: Is there anyone you feel more connected with since your trauma?

Client: Well, my dog, as strange as that might sound. I realized that my dog is the only one that is always there for me, not judging, just loving.

Therapist: What difference has that made in your life?

Client: In a weird way, I feel as if I am OK; as if I am loved and lovable. I don't think I ever really felt OK before this. If the trauma is what it took to get that sense, I guess it was worth it. Although I never want to go through anything like that again, I can tell you.

5.2.2 Investigate Increases in Compassion and Empathy in the Wake of the Trauma

I heard rock musician Peter Gabriel talk about having been sexually assaulted by classmates when he was a young boy. After it happened, he didn't tell anybody. It was swept under the rug. He felt ashamed and powerless.

Many years later, he was asked to go on a music tour to raise money for Amnesty International. During that tour, he met people who had seen loved ones tortured or thrown out of airplanes, and who had been tortured themselves. But what really moved him was that after these terrible experiences, their suffering and the crimes that were committed were denied and suppressed. He said, "From my privileged position, the only way I could relate to these stories was through my experience of having been abused and then having it denied and suppressed afterwards. And I couldn't turn away in quite the same way I had before." His own trauma increased his empathy.

Therapist: Is there any way in which going through this has put you in touch with more compassion?

Client: Well, I think I have more heart for anyone who is suffering. When the tsunami happened, it was all I could do to keep myself from quitting my job and going over there to help. I sent more money than I could afford, really, but it felt good. I know what it is like to suffer and I find it harder these days to shut out the suffering of others.

. . . .

Client: I had never considered coming to therapy before. I thought people who went to therapists were a bunch of pathetic whiners who blamed their parents for every little problem they had.

Therapist: And now?

Client: Well, I was wrong. Since this happened to me, I realize I was very judgmental. Because I had never faced anything I couldn't handle before, I felt pretty superior. But now I've been humbled. Everybody has to ask for help sometime. Nobody is Superman.

5.2.3 Investigate Increased Activity in the Areas of Service and Contribution in the Aftermath of Trauma

Because people often feel more compassionate toward the suffering of others after they go through and survive a trauma, they might feel moved to do some volunteer work, take up a cause, or make some other positive contribution to the world or other people.

In this section the dialogue will illustrate investigating this area of contribution and service arising from trauma.

Therapist: Do you volunteer or do any charitable work?

.   .   .   .

Therapist: Is there any area in which you think you could contribute in the world?

.   .   .   .

Therapist: Do you have the sense that this trauma has clarified your purpose for being alive?

Client: I think I need to become more active in creating safe bicycle routes since my wife's accident. It isn't right that more people are probably going to die needlessly because there aren't safe areas for people to ride their bikes in this city.

We have taken a quick trip through four alternative treatments to trauma and I have to remind readers once again that these aren't the "right" ways to treat trauma, only some ways that haven't been part of the mainstream that I and my clients have found useful.

Since many people who come to therapists have not been helped, we cannot afford to be doctrinaire in our approaches. We are searching for what works for this particular person at this particular time. In my view, nothing works for everyone all the time. This is what makes psychotherapy both so challenging and rewarding. We are always working with an N of 1, as they say in experimental work.

I have tried to make the book very simple and readable, since all too many therapy books are thick, filled with jargon, and remain sitting by the side of the bed, unread past the first chapter. But I hope this simplicity did not hide the fact that a lot of deep thinking and hard work gave rise to these ideas and methods.

If what you have read in this book helps alleviate the suffering of even one person, I will have considered it a success. Thank you for taking the time to consider these ideas.

Appendix: Posttraumatic Success Scales

What follows are some rating scales that you can use to help you and your clients assess where they are in their posttraumatic success. I offer these scales as potentially helpful tools, not as definitive or scientifically validated instruments.

Indeed, this a good sensibility with which to conclude the book. I have offered all these ideas, methods, and tools as possibilities, rather than doctrinaire truths and dictums. It seems to me that such an attitude is important given that we, as clinicians, don't help every traumatized person who seeks our help, or we only help them partially. As a field, I hope we are always open to new ideas and methods that can help us be more effective at relieving the considerable suffering that arises from human cruelty and unpreventable tragedies.

To hearken back to the incident that sparked this book (the mental health expert pronouncing that people affected by the 9/11 attacks would "never get over it"): People can and do get over trauma, but not everyone does. If anything in this book has helped you be more effective with even one traumatized client, I will consider your time and mine well spent.

Thank you for taking the time and attention, precious commodities in our all-too-busy days, to consider these ideas and methods.

Put a check mark or an X in the column that applies after each item.

Table A.1   The Connection Scale

	Not at all or rarely	Sometimes	Often or usually	Very often or very much
I feel connected to my body.				
I feel connected to my inner self/intuition/soul/spirit.				
I feel connected to at least one other person (family member, friend, co-worker, team member, boyfriend/ girlfriend/partner).				
I feel connected to a pet or animal I own.				
I feel connected to a group of friends.				
I feel connected to nature.				
I feel connected to something beyond myself.				
I connect to myself or something beyond myself through experiencing art.				
I connect to myself or something beyond myself through creating art.				
I feel connected to some spiritual sense or power.				
I feel as if my life has meaning or purpose.				

Table A.2 The Compassion Scale

	Not at all or rarely	Sometimes	Often or usually	Very often or very much
I feel empathy for others.				
I feel sympathy for others.				
I am touched by the suffering of animals.				
I am touched by the suffering of people.				
I feel accepting of the flaws and foibles of others.				
I feel love and kindness toward others or humanity in general.				

Table A.3 The Contribution Scale

	Not at all or rarely	Sometimes	Often or usually	Very often or very much
I donate to charitable causes.				
I do something to help others.				
I try to make the world a better place.				
I do something to solve problems for others or the world.				
My work or my life contributes to the betterment of the lives of others.				
I am of service to others.				

References

American Psychiatric Association. (2000.) *Diagnostic and statistical manual of mental disorders, dsm-iv-tr fourth edition (text revision)*. Washington, DC: Author.

Armenian, H., et. al. (2000). Loss as a determinant of PTSD in a cohort of adult survivors of the 1998 earthquake in Armenia: Implications for policy. *Acta Psychiatr. Scand., 102*: 58–64.

Barbash, T. (2006, September 11). A tale of renewal: For the 9/11 survivors of Cantor Fitzgerald, working to rebuild their firm has been the key to healing. Retrieved from http://www.businessweek.com/print/magazine/content/06_37/b4000077.htm?chan=gl

Bonanno, G., Wortman, C., Lehman, D., Tweed, R., Haring, M., Sonnega, J., Carr, D., and Nesse, R. (2002). Resilience to loss and chronic grief: A prospective study from preloss to 18-months postloss. *Journal of Social Issues, 83*: 1150–64.

Bonnano, G. A., Rennicke, C., and Dekel, S. (2005). Self-enhancement among high-exposure survivors of the September 11th terrorist attack: Resilience or social maladjustment? *Journal of Personality and Social Psychology, 88*: 984–88.

Breslau, N., Kessler, R., Chilcoat, H., Schultz, L., Davis, G., and Andreski, P. (1998). Trauma and post-traumatic stress disorder in the community: The 1996 Detroit Area Survey of Trauma. *Archive of General Psychiatry, 55*(7): 626–32.

Browne, I. (1990). Psychological trauma, or unexperienced experience. *Re-vision, 12*(4): 21.

Burns, G. (1998). *Nature guided therapy: Brief integrative strategies for health and well being*. New York: Brunner/Mazel.

Carver, C. S. (1998). Resilience and thriving: Issues, models and linkages. *Journal of Social Issues, 54*: 245–66.

Doidge, N. (2007). *The brain that changes itself*. New York: Penguin.

Frumkin, H. (2001). Beyond toxicity: Human health and the natural environment. *American Journal of Preventative Medicine, 20*(3): 234–40.

Kessler, R. C., Sonnega, A., Bromet, E., Hughes, M., and Nelson, C. B. (1995). Trauma and post-traumatic stress disorder in the National Comorbidity Survey. *Archive of General Psychiatry, 52*(12):1048–60.

Lepore, S. J., and Smyth, J. M. (Eds.) (2002). *The writing cure: How expressive writing promotes health and emotional well-being.* Washington, DC: American Psychiatric Association.

Linley, P. A., and Joseph, S. (2004). Positive change following trauma and adversity: A review. *Journal of Traumatic Stress, 17:* 11–21.

Pennebaker, J. (1990). *Opening up: The healing power of expressing emotions.* New York: Guilford.

Shapiro, F. (1995). *Eye movement desensitization and reprocessing: Basic principles, protocols, and procedures.* New York: Guilford.

Smith, T. C., Ryan, A. K., Wingard, D. L., Slymen, D. J., Sallis, J. F., Kritz-Silverstein, D. & the Millennium Cohort Study Team. (2008). New onset and persistent symptoms of post-traumatic stress disorder self reported after deployment and combat exposures: Prospective population based US military cohort study. *BMJ, 336*(7640): 366–371.

Tedeschi, R. G., and Calhoun, L. G. (1996). The Posttraumatic Growth Inventory: Measuring the positive legacy of trauma. *Journal of Traumatic Stress, 9*(3): 455–71.

Tedeschi, R. G., and Calhoun, L. G. (2004). Posttraumatic growth: Conceptual foundations and empirical evidence. *Psychological Inquiry, 15:* 1–18.

Veterans Administration. (2007, August 26). Facing combat without stress? Researchers examine most resilient soldiers. *VA News Flash.* Retrieved from http://articles.courant.com/2007–08–25/news/0708250559_1_combat-stress-psychological-trauma-mental-health